THE RISE OF THE HUMANS

The vision-driven approach to life that
lifts you up to the heights of fulfilment

Dr. Homi Azemikhah

Copyright © 2025 Dr. Homi Azemikhah. All rights reserved. No portion of this book, except for brief review, may be reproduced, stored in a retrieval system, or transmitted in any form or by any means—electronic, mechanical, photocopying, recording, or otherwise—without the written permission of the publisher.

Published by
Inspired Publishing Ltd
27 Old Gloucester Street
London
WC1N 3AX

Printed in the United Kingdom, United States and Australia

ISBN : 978-1-78555-125-3

Dedication

This work is dedicated to the following:
To my mother, Tooran, who inspired me to write it,
To the mothers of readers who have chosen to rise to the heights of fulfilment by discovering, planning, and fulfilling their Life's Vision.

I also, dedicate this poem to all mothers

Life is tough
Mother's ♥ love ♥ makes it soft
Life is empty
Mother's ♥ love ♥ makes it full
Life is hurt
Mother's ♥ love ♥ makes it heal
Life is sad
Mother's ♥ love ♥ makes it happy
Life is fear
Mother's ♥ love ♥ makes it safe
Life is lone
Mother's ♥ love ♥ makes it together
Life is anger
Mother's ♥ love ♥ makes it calm
Life is unfair
Mother's ♥ love ♥ makes it fair
Because…
Life doesn't come with a manual
It comes with a mother

THE RISE OF THE HUMANS

Table of Contents

Dedication 3
Foreword 7
Preface 9
Introduction 13

Chapter 1
Life's Vision 19

Chapter 2
The Promise 47

Chapter 3
Our talents and what we love. 87

Chapter 4
Rise of The Humans Framework (ROTH) 125

Chapter 5
How to work with ROTH 171

Chapter 6
Discovering your Life's Vision and Personal Constitution 215

Chapter 7
Four stories on Life's Vision 239

Chapter 8
The Directional Vision Board and its significance 251

Chapter 9
Develop Mastery in Visional Planning 279

Chapter 10
Your Time Has Come 313
About the author 319

THE RISE OF THE HUMANS

Foreword

The author draws on substantial experience in teaching competency-based training. He has combined 20 years of training together with his research experience in creating a simple readable format of how competent the readers can become in discovering and fulfiling of their Life's Vision.

It is now well established that our Life's Vision is so important, as your life vision is something you love and have the talents and skills to do it well. Your Life's Vision is also supported by your values.

The author, Dr. Homi, known as Dr. Competence, has portrayed how applying these 3 components of what you love to do, your talents, and the values that are important for you in your life can converge and inspire you to discover your life's true vision.

He then takes you on the journey of the vision-driven path to plan and fulfil your Life's Vision. He has introduced a new approach in creating your Life's Vision board with the direction your Life's Vision indicates. He has been innovating, creative and inventive in his approach that for the first time presents the idea of the arrow of vision. He then teaches how by placing your life's arrow of vision in the middle of the Life's Vision board you give your vision board the direction it needs to guide you to fulfilment. He has called it the Directional Vision Board (DVB) on the premise that your Life's Vision must become the basis of your vision board, not the New Year's Resolution that is customary as it lapses every year.

He then takes you through a new way of planning that can be drawn and tattooed to your face based on Ta Moko principles practiced by the Māori people of New Zealand. He then humorously explains that your plan is tattooed to an image of your face, not your real face. This important planning you do on your face becomes a commitment to yourself to carry out the plan to its fulfilment.

The book emphasises that the only way to escape from the pain of regrets because of not fulfilling your Life's Vision, is to take action to discover and fulfil your Life's Vision before it is too late and before the pain of regrets kicks in. When the pain of regrets starts to kick into your life there is no going back, and it is too late. The pain will stay for years to come and beyond. It is the most important thing you must do in your life and if you don't beware, you can't escape the claws of the pain of regrets.

He introduces you to your Life's Vision Board, this is unique, and it is the first book of this kind, as no book so far has spoken about Life's Vision board with your life's arrow of vision, call it directional Vision Board as it is your Life's Vision that gives you your direction.

I recommend The Rise of The Humans as a good read to tackle the question of what my Life's Vision is and how I can fulfil it before it is too late and before the pain of regrets kicks in. This book has the potential to transform your life.

Pat Mesiti

Preface

In every chapter of the book, you come across the word 'Life's Vision' and its many secrets. These secrets will be unravelled and unfolded throughout the book. When you discover these secrets leading subsequently to your Life's Vision, your life will never be the same again. Everything you see around you has been once someone's Life's Vision, and now they are part of the reality. Just imagine that yours would be among them one day and its fulfilment brings fortunes, happiness, success, and satisfaction.

If you miss, delay or postpone, the opportunity of discovering and fulfilling your Life's Vision, you face the most severe and debilitating pain, the pain of regrets. You will learn the secret of avoiding the pain of regrets before it is too late and before the pain of regrets kicks in.

The highest secret that everyone has intrinsically endowed with is their Life's Vision. Your Life's Vision is likened to a pearl hidden in a shell in the dept of an ocean waiting to be discovered. You will learn how to dive into that great ocean to reach this pearl and let its value be known to the world, and let the world around you benefit therefrom; this is your happiness, your fulfilment.

As I became an expert in the world on the subject of competence and qualified after 10 years of research and 20 years of teaching, I saw the opportunity to apply my expertise to this most important topic, Life's Vision and help those who don't know how to discover it competently, articulate it competently, plan it competently and fulfil it competently.

In doing so I have researched how great visionaries applied these secrets and made fortunes. Like Steve Jobs, Mark Zuckerberg and Jack Ma, while others like Helen Keller discovered and fulfilled their Life's Vision to help the cause of the blind. While Gandhi discovered and fulfilled his Life's Vision to free India. You will learn how the ripples from the butterfly effect of Gandhi's Life's Vision reached Nelson Mandela and Martin Luther King years later and transformed those lands.

These names represent a fraction of visionaries whose fulfilment led from fortunes to freedom.

The cause they had was their Life's Vision and without their Life's Vision it was impossible to achieve what they did.

As a reader you are in the same position as Steve Jobs, Jack Ma, Helen Keller, Mark Zuckerberg and Gandhi and those who discovered and fulfilled their Life's Vision in the past. You will learn from examples of Gandhi, Hellen Keller, Jack Ma, Steve Jobs Mark Zuckerberg and their secrets.

Somewhere in the book you will find your own secret, the missing link. It could be when you discover your gifts, what you love truly and some values that are important to you that you didn't know about. Something that you didn't know before it clicks and pops up in your mind, becomes your AHA moment.

When you grasp the meaning of your AHA moment, and when this happens, it is such an important moment as it reveals who you are, and you won't believe that you could have ever discovered it, but you did. By grasping the meaning of your AHA moment, you will never be the same again.

Preface

At that moment, turn a glass upside down, and on paper write, "Thank God, I finally Got It". Write the date and time and leave the note under the glass for a while. Take a photo of the glass and make sure the note is visible in the photo. Keep the photo and send it to yourself in a message or email congratulating yourself for discovering your Life's Vision.

Welcome to the club, welcome on board, because now you understand how you feel when you discover it, how emotional it is, how touching it is, and how it brings tears to your eyes, the time of Gladness and Sadness has arrived. Gladness because you finally got it, and Sadness, because you may think why you did not discover it years earlier. This mix of emotions will remain with you till the end that has no end.

Because, at that AHA moment, your life is transformed, and you can never forget it. Because You have realised the simple fact that Steve Jobs has been talking about and Helen Keller emphasised. You will realise that you will never be the same again.

Dr Homi Azemikhah

THE RISE OF THE HUMANS

Introduction

Rise of the Robots is a myth. If you type, "Rise of the Robots is a myth" into a search engine like Google, you will have over 5 million hits. Many websites and authentic sources disagree with the doctrine in the book "Rise of the Robots". Here, in my book, is the case for what I call the Rise of the Humans. According to Chris Richardson, one of Australia's most respected economists and a partner at Deloitte, the largest professional services network in the world by revenue and number of professionals and one of the "big four" accounting firms, "robots are used for the repetitive and boring jobs of the future". These are what I call the jobs for the hands.

In my earlier book, "Create Your Mental GPS" I referred to the importance of equilibrium between the work we do with our hands, and the work we do with our minds while being inspired by our hearts.

An important difference between humans and robots is that humans have a Vision, for their lives for their futures, but robots do not. While the concept described in the book Rise of the Robots is a myth, the ideas in my book, Rise of the Humans are facts. The time has come now for the Rise of the Humans, and I will contribute to facilitating this through the message contained in the pages of this book. As you read on, you will observe the process of your own metamorphosis, whilst in the cocoon of vision, as a jaw-dropping experience leading to the emergence of a new you. You will discover during this process, how your vision, a gift/ability that robots do not have, empowers you to rise (up, through the levels I will describe later), to the heights of fulfilment, through the energies released by your own metamorphosis.

The time has come to rise as humans and fulfil what we are here to fulfil in our life. Part of this process of fulfilment is about our job, our work, our business, our goals, our dreams and so forth. But all that we call our job or our work, business, dreams and so on involves applying the use of our heads, hands and hearts.

The jobs for our heads, which include new inventions and discoveries in scientific research, and especially the jobs for our hearts, are the jobs for humans, and the demand for these jobs is rising. In fact, the "Rise of the Robots" has inadvertently caused an increased awareness, among most of us, about the jobs for humans, and this is contributing to the increased overall awareness of the rise of humans now and continuing into the future.

The pivot around which the Rise of the Humans rotates is "Service". Service is connected to our hearts and delivered through heartfelt endeavours. It requires that as humans we adopt the "Spirit of Service" in what we do (our jobs, our work, our businesses, etc.) in our lives. The spirit of service is delivered through the link from our hearts as humans and via the spirit of oneness that we share with those we serve, such as our customers and clients who are scattered around the world and hence bringing about a global oneness awareness, the likes of which no one has experienced before now because of the advances in technology available to us all today. This profound awareness pivots around our Life's Vision.

Introduction

It is a sense of relief that comes over us when on the other side of the phone call we hear a human voice not a robot, as the heart connects with hearts in an invisible global network of humans, as we all rise as humans in this still relatively new millennium. This is why the concept of the rise of the robots to take our jobs is actually a myth. In addition, every advance in technology brings about a great number of new opportunities that result in new jobs being created.

Humans connection is about the jobs of the hearts, which as I mentioned earlier are rising in demand now and into the future. The spirit of service around which customer service revolves is on the rise, in terms of its use and popularity, and with it, the rise of humans. The pivot around which the rise of the humans is taking place is service. It is the spirit of service that lifts us up (metaphorically, because of the sense of fulfilment that we feel when we give heartfelt service) when it is delivered via our Life's Vision (meaning our life purpose) to serve humankind.

As robots do not have vision (a life's purpose to which they feel connected to), they also have no regrets (the negative emotion that they should have made a different decision in the past to avoid disappointment in the present) when things go wrong. However, as humans we need to be aware of the risk of regrets that could come about later in life, if we disregard our Life's Vision, as our Life's Vision is the reason for our being here in this life. Every human being has a specific vision that is within them and needs to be discovered and fulfilled within their lifetime. By finding our vision, we begin our journey of realising our dreams and thus we avoid the circumstances that usually lead to feeling regret when approaching the later years of our life. By stepping onto the vision-driven path and following our vision, being inspired by it, and moving towards its fulfilment, we start to feel we are rising to the heights of fulfilment, as humans, on the journey towards our ultimate fulfilment.

This book, "The Rise of the Humans" provides a profound philosophy and approach to illustrating how humans are able to rise, metaphorically, around the spirit of service globally and how this spirit of service is connected, via our vision, to oneness with our customers, clients, neighbours, friends, and communities around the world.

I share the story of my mother who was unable to fulfil her dream of becoming a surgeon and midwife, and the consequence of not fulfilling her Life's Vision, at the start of the book.

This book places a profound emphasis on the importance of our Life's Vision. Every human being is endowed with a Life's Vision, and the spirit of service a possibility. This possibility means humans can become global beings by sharing their Life's Vision. With the advances in technology, the horizons of service have been broadened. So, it is now possible for us to serve the world from our homes, or indeed from any place we choose.

In this context, I call upon all human beings to come together, to rise as humans, by fulfilling their own Life's Visions. Fulfilling our Life's Vision is vital. Accomplishing it in our life is crucial. By digging deep within and discovering our Life's Vision, our single most important role in this life becomes clear. It is to bring that vision to fruition through the spirit of service. Accomplishing this elevates us to higher levels of becoming visionary and embracing the world with our Life's Vision.

Introduction

On this journey of fulfilment, issues and problems may arise. The Rise of the Humans Framework (ROTH) presented in Chapter 4, illustrates how we are able to deal with any issues that may occur, and how by pursuing our Life's Vision we can reach the level where we can adopt the spirit of service in our lives where we become empowered and enabled to serve the world (Customers, clients, people) around us in a simple and profound way to fulfilment.

On this basis, the book's doctrine focuses on the notion that everyone has the opportunity to reach the level of service. Then, they can continue to serve by adopting the Spirit of Service. Then, they can activate the spirit of oneness: oneness with people around them, their clients, their customers, followers and fans worldwide.

This book calls on all humans to discover and fulfil their Life's Vision by Rising to the level of Spirit of Service and Spirit of Oneness. This invitation is to all humans as members of one body of humanity worldwide, business owners, professionals, politicians, teachers, students, all people. It is inclusive to embrace everyone. Why? Because, the time has come for us as Human beings, as one human Race to Rise by discovering and fulfilling our Life's Vision. The time of fulfilment, and rising as a human has come.

THE RISE OF THE HUMANS

Chapter 1
Life's Vision

"The only thing worse than being blind is having sight but no vision" Helen Keller

Helen Keller was blind; she knew the disadvantage of having no sight, yet she emphasised that the lack of vision is worse than being blind. If the lack of vision in our life is worse than being blind, then we need to be serious about discovering, and articulating our Life's Vision. The vision-driven approach presented in the chapters of this book provides you with several easy and practical steps to discover, articulate and fulfil your Life's Vision.

We manifest a sense of rising fulfilment as we go through these steps. At each stage, we rise higher and higher until we feel that we are at the heights of fulfilment. In such a state, we see ourselves carrying the feeling of fulfilment in our life before we reach the end. We find peace, tranquillity, success, and happiness. By reaching such a state of mind, we experience rising every day of our life, higher and higher that we couldn't have imagined when we started. Steve Jobs's reference to finding our vision is very empowering.

As Steve Jobs put it,

> "When you grow up, you tend to get told that the world is the way it is. And your life is just to live your life inside the world, try not to bash into the walls too much, try to have a nice family life, have fun, save little money. But that's a very limited life. Life can be

much broader, once you discover one simple fact and that is: Everything around you that you call life was made up by people that were not smarter than you. And you can change it, you can influence it, you can mould it, you can build your own things that other people can use. And, the minute that you understand, that you can poke life in, actually, something you know you push in, something will pop out the other side. You can change it. You can mould it. That may be the most important thing, is to shake off this erroneous notion that life is there and you're just gonna live in it, versus embrace it, change it, improve it, make your mark upon it. I think that is very important. Once you learn that, you'll wanna change life and make it better because it's kinda messed up in a lot of ways. Once you learn that, you will never be the same again".

How can you discover the simple fact that Steve Jobs is talking about? Discovering your Life's Vision, is not only a journey of transformation but a journey of influencing the world around you when you are able to turn your vision into reality. When you can build your life around your vision, and when you fulfil your Life's Vision, you will never be the same again. As both Helen Keller and Steve Jobs have elucidated: Everyone's vision is unique within that individual waiting to be discovered and fulfilled. You are given unique talents to be nurtured and developed to be used to fulfil that vision. At the outset you may question whether this might be your Life's Vision, but soon, you will see, it will be. You are here in this life to fulfil your Life's Vision, of serving humanity, the world, and mankind. For the welfare of humankind, the vision that is within you is needed. It needs to be mined and fulfilled.

In other words, bringing out our talents and what we love, in service to our customers, clients and humanity depends on discovering our vision in this life. By discovering, and fulfilling it, we contribute to the advancement of humanity. Within the fulfilment of our Life's Vision lies the secrets of wealth, riches, fame, success and accomplishment, discoveries, inventions, and so forth. Until fulfilment is attained, people are confused about what to do in this world and in their lives, and some have even asked "why are we here?" because they do not know.

We need to discover Life's Vision as it is inner. When we discover it, it excites us. It wakes us up. It moves us and makes us make it happen. By doing something we have never thought of before, we can create something we could never have imagined creating or accomplishing. That is what our vision, i.e., our Life's Vision is all about. There are strong reasons why we must discover, achieve, and fulfil it. The strongest reason in the whole universe is that it is our Life's Vision, and we know deep down that it is the only reason we are here; to fulfil the vision of becoming who we truly are, our Life's Vision.

The three things that are unique about us as humans and exist in each one of us are: our talents, what we love, and the set of values that we hold dear in our hearts. Our vision is where these three things converge and it, differs from individual to individual. We can change and influence the people around us. How can we do that? We can do it by discovering our Life's Vision first. By discovering our Life's Vision, we realise that, not only does it help us fulfil our life, but it also helps the people around us, and humanity in general to prosper. In fact, the whole universe will be able to go one step further and engage in the larger fulfilment, the fulfilment of humanity, the fulfilment of the human race.

You have heard that Steve Jobs successfully designed Apple computers, iPhones, and all their other products. Apple computers became the first trillion Dollar Company in the world. It all started with Steve's "Simple Fact" and from a small garage. His simple fact transformed into his Life's Vision to serve Humanity through new designs for computers and smartphones was fulfilled. Now whenever we hear his name, we see Apple smartphones and computers in our minds.

If we are not on this journey of rising fulfilment, the alternative is a life that ends up with regrets. The question is how can we live a life of rising fulfilment? How can we rise, rise some more, and keep rising for as long as we live, until we reach the heights of fulfilment? This book provides the answers.

Whom this book is written for:

- New business start-ups who need to be aware of the significance of Vision and Cashflow.
- Businesspeople who are struggling with their business.
- Students at risk of non-completion and on the verge of quitting studies.
- Big corporations who have difficulty aligning staff with strategic planning to accomplish the corporate vision.

- Universities, institutes, and colleges, to boost their student-completion rates by bringing attention to the significance of Life's Vision
- For everyone whose vision is important for them to accomplish, to learn to fully uncover/discover it, plan it, fulfil it, and to rise as a human in the process.

So, are you ready to begin? Okay, then. Let's start with the V, which stands for Vision and Values. Look at the following tree: the Tree of Vision or Vision Tree. Its branches are made of the values in your life. In other words, what you value. Our life brings about our vision. The fruit of the tree of vision is fulfilment. The fruit of our Life's Vision, in the beginning, is in the seed. The leaves on the tree of vision are the benefits that can multiply and become plentiful. These benefits include happiness, peace, and abundance, which are values, and whatever you value and desire to be abundant in your life, money, wealth, joy, and desired relationships. The roots are our talents, and what we love to do, wishes, desires and wants, and even hopes. The simple presentation of the Tree of Vision or Vision Tree is illustrated in Figure 1.1. The extended version of Tree of Vision will be introduced in later chapters. Our desires, passions, talents, things we love to do, wishes and dreams strengthen the root. Values of excitement, enthusiasm, persistent dedication and more are found in the upper part of the tree in the branches and make the vision tree grow and become verdant.

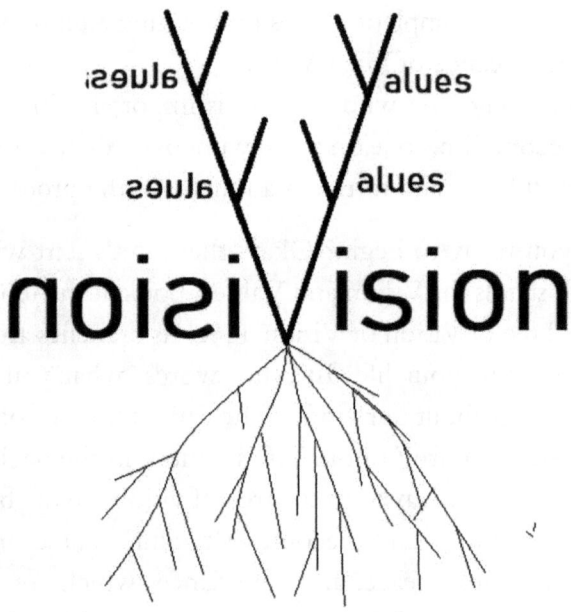

Figure 1.1 – Vision Tree

Do you feel everyone wants to direct you in your life? Are you tired of being directed by hundreds of approaches? Approaches to self-fulfilment? Money-making? Achieving success? Happiness? Does it feel as if each method is dragging you in a different direction, which is not yours?

If so, you are not alone, and there are a few basic facts that significantly benefit you. Firstly, do you know that you are in fact your own direction? Do you know that you are better off, going in the direction of your Life's Vision than following anyone else's vision? Where do you think you can find the best answers to these questions in your life? Where are the secrets to your Life's Vision? Do you know that the

Life's Vision

secret to your life's Vision and direction are within you? You will learn about these secrets in the following chapters.

Then the question is where within you do you find it? Because, within you there are hundreds, even thousands, of ideas, wishes, desires, wants, thoughts, and so on. Where exactly and which one is the answer? However, sometimes in life we are doubtful as to what to do, so there are moments when choosing which way to go, when we come to a fork in the road, is difficult.

When you need answers, do you like to go within yourself, to your center, to find the answers? If so, I have a treat in store for you. Are you ready for such a journey of adventure? If the answer is yes, let's pack your bags and get ready for our trip. If this is your first time, you are in for a treat too. Let's go on a profound journey to find all the answers. Let's solve the issues that are bothering and stopping you from finding your vision and direction in life. Do you know that all the answers and secrets are within you? Well, they are! If you have never thought of that before, take a moment to imagine it… imagine getting answers to your life's most essential questions from within yourself. Can you see now that this is an entirely new game? Can you see that this is a new approach to creating certainty in your life, which is waiting to begin unfolding?

At the outset, you need to ask yourself several questions of certainty to discover where you are in your life. You need to be ready with absolute certainty. This book takes you where you have never been before. There, you will find your uniqueness, your greatness, and your significance. You will take a journey to an ocean within yourself to discover those answers, and as you do so, you will pick up new gems of understanding and new answers and your life will start to make more sense and become more meaningful as you continue. As the level of meaningfulness increases on this journey of self-exploration, you will start to feel lighter and start feeling as if you are rising. This feeling of rising increases and you find you are rising higher and higher; you start to get the feeling of fulfilment and contentment as you rise and you will become clearer with a vivid life direction as you reach above and go beyond the answers to those questions of certainty.

Next, a Quick Exercise:

Answer the following question: How certain are you about your direction and your Life's Vision right now?

How certain are you?	10	20	30	40	50	60	70	80	90	100
Place a tick ⇨										

Ask yourself; how are you going about your life now? As human beings, we need to be certain of our direction in life. Are you sure the direction you are taking is the right direction? Are you certain? How do you know you are heading in the right direction? This is the right time to deal with the questions of certainty in your life and the direction your life is taking. This certainty of direction is important, and I will explain why shortly.

Are you confident about what you are doing (in your life) right now, and about your direction in life? Do you see that the problems in your life can be directly or indirectly related to certainty of direction? Reflect on where the connection is between this certainty and problems in your life.

Life's Vision

When you become uncertain about your health, you check with a doctor. When you are uncertain about something you want to do you may check on the internet. When you are not certain about the meaning of a word, you check the dictionary, right? After doing any of the above, you become certain and then you continue with life until the next time you feel uncertain again. Then everything is on hold until you clarify or clear away the uncertainties. Do you know that the more certain you are about your direction, the more confident you will become? Yes, you are right if your answer is yes, because certainty is the mother of confidence and competence. This is why certainty is so important.

Focus on the following questions of certainty. Reflect and rate your certainty by ticking the appropriate boxes between 10% and 100%?

How certain are you about your direction in life?

How certain are you?	10	20	30	40	50	60	70	80	90	100
Place a tick ⇨										

Are you certain that you are moving forward with passion and enthusiasm in your life?

How certain are you?	10	20	30	40	50	60	70	80	90	100
Place a tick ⇨										

Are you certain that you are developing your knowledge and skills?

How certain are you?	10	20	30	40	50	60	70	80	90	100
Place a tick ⇨										

As human beings, we need to grow daily, even hourly and in every minute of our life. Are you certain that you are growing?

How certain are you?	10	20	30	40	50	60	70	80	90	100
Place a tick ⇨										

Are you certain that you are growing in the right direction?

How certain are you?	10	20	30	40	50	60	70	80	90	100
Place a tick ⇨										

Are you certain that you are feeling fulfilled? Do you feel certain that the direction you are heading leads to fulfilment?

How certain are you?	10	20	30	40	50	60	70	80	90	100
Place a tick ⇨										

Are you certain that direction will contribute to your community, society, or humanity?

How certain are you?	10	20	30	40	50	60	70	80	90	100
Place a tick ⇨										

Are you certain that your direction and efforts are based on your values, talents and what you love to do in life?

How certain are you?	10	20	30	40	50	60	70	80	90	100
Place a tick ⇨										

Are you certain about what makes you unique?

How certain are you?	10	20	30	40	50	60	70	80	90	100
Place a tick ⇨										

Are you certain about your significance/importance /relevance?

How certain are you?	10	20	30	40	50	60	70	80	90	100
Place a tick ⇨										

Are you certain of your beliefs, and core values?

How certain are you?	10	20	30	40	50	60	70	80	90	100
Place a tick ⇨										

Life's Vision

How certain are you about serving your clients, customers, people around you, your family, your community?

How certain are you?	10	20	30	40	50	60	70	80	90	100
Place a tick ⇨										

How certain are you about accepting yours and others' strengths and weaknesses?

How certain are you?	10	20	30	40	50	60	70	80	90	100
Place a tick ⇨										

How certain are you about new opportunities and new ideas?

How certain are you?	10	20	30	40	50	60	70	80	90	100
Place a tick ⇨										

How certain are you about sociability and that you are connecting with your audience?

How certain are you?	10	20	30	40	50	60	70	80	90	100
Place a tick ⇨										

How certain are you about being present?

How certain are you?	10	20	30	40	50	60	70	80	90	100
Place a tick ⇨										

How certain are you about dealing with your fears?

How certain are you?	10	20	30	40	50	60	70	80	90	100
Place a tick ⇨										

So far, while we have been reading through the above questions of certainty, we may have experienced many thoughts popping up, as we reflected on these questions of certainty we realise that:

- As human beings we need to feel free and be certain that we are growing, moving forward, expanding, developing, and that we are not uncertain, stagnant, and strained.
- Being unclear on certainty of direction creates other uncertainties.
- As human beings we want to be certain of our direction and where we are heading in our lives.
- The most important certainty in our lives is the certainty of direction. This certainty is only delineated by our Life's Vision. It is our Life's Vision that provides us with such a clarity.

However, before discovering our Life's Vision, we must know that:
- Our higher self has laid down a unique life vision for us to follow and unless we discover and pursue that vision, we will inevitably raise a conflict within ourselves throughout our life that leads us to feeling regretful in the end. Our regrets and internal conflicts arise when we are uncertain about our Life's Vision, and we take a different direction in our lives than our inner vision suggests. Our internal conflicts arise throughout our lives we feel that we are not growing. Our regrets arise when we feel that we are not fulfilled, or we may develop fears of not being able to be fulfilled or we may feel that we are not going in the right direction towards fulfilment. This gives rise to our disappointments. These disappointments lead to the feeling of not contributing to ourselves, the community, and the world around us. Our regrets become stronger when, as a result, we do not feel

significant about ourselves and what we are doing. So, what is the solution?

- Our Life's Vision is something that we need to discover within ourselves, and when we discover our Life's Vision, it excites us and makes us move; it wakes us up from our slumber. It moves us and makes us make it happen. By doing something we have never thought before, we can create something we could never have thought to create before. That is what our Life's Vision do for us. There are strong reasons why we must achieve, and fulfil it. The strongest reason in the whole universe is that it is our Life's Vision, and we own it as our most valuable asset ever, and we know deep down that the only reason we are here is to fulfil that vision, our Life's Vision.

- We are here in this life to become our vision, this is the process of becoming, this is who we are, and we must act to make our vision materialise, because by following and fulfilling our vision, we become who we really are meant to become, and at the end we become our vision. We have come to this life to begin the journey of becoming our vision, becoming who we really are. By becoming, we have answered the question of who we are.

After we discover our Life's Vision, the vision for our life, this is how we feel:

- When we discover our Life's Vision, we will be living a life of passion and commitment that is free of internal conflicts and regrets, and we feel we want to rise. We will be living a life of certainty, a life of joy where we have come to experience our greatness, and

our significance in our life and we feel that we are rising. We feel great with an aura of certainty about our direction, and these make us rise. Then, we realise that our confidence is rising, and a sense of rising fulfilment constantly fills our souls.
- When we discover our vision and live it, we will be living a life in which we contribute to society with certainty, we contribute to our community, or the world with joy and whilst feeling proud, we start to feel a warm sense of satisfaction flowing through our veins and our entire being.
- The joy we experience on this journey is an extremely unique experience and gives us a sense of significance that is hard to put into words. The joy has a unique quality of its own that is linked to our uniqueness. It is a joy that makes us rise higher, and higher, and higher as a human being. As we start to rise, we get a feeling, of being lifted, higher and higher to our bliss.
- Then we realise that there is a nexus between fulfilling our Life's Vision and rising as a human. The closer we are to fulfilling our Life's Vision, the higher we rise as a human. The closer we are to the realisation of our Life's Vision, the higher we rise as a human. The higher we rise, the more we feel fulfilment of our Life's Vision. It is an upward spiral of feeling, moving higher and rising higher, resulting in reciprocal empowerment.

What we need to be aware of doing in our life:
- It is of the utmost importance to find out what our Life's Vision is. We do this by communicating with

our higher self, laying down the required plan, and performing the required actions, to fulfil it. Accomplishing this also requires us to apply perseverance and determination to whatever it takes. The joy radiating from the fulfilment of our Life's Vision is so immensely empowering that we feel its energy vibrating and illuminating our entire being. It is difficult to explain in only a few words. Soon, we discover that our sole purpose for being here on this planet, and in this life, has been to find our Life's Vision. To explain further, we quickly realise that we are born to this life to discover our vision, become certain about it, and that our sole duty, which we owe to ourselves to fulfil, is our Life's Vision. When we start this journey, sooner or later, it becomes clear that our life has been that vision. And we further realise that we are here to live in accordance with the fulfilment of that vision, our Life's Vision. In the end, we become our vision'. Hence, if we reflect, we realise that our life is our vision and we become our vision at the end of this life. The point is that if we need to become our vision to fulfil our life, we must find it, live it, and become it.

- It also becomes clear to us how we feel as we are lifted. That is, we will realise that when we follow our inner voice, or our higher self, we rise higher. As humans, we rise higher when we follow the advice of our own inner voice, and higher self, in pursuit of our Life's Vision, and about what our vision is, not the vision of others. When we adhere to the advice of our inner voice and Higher self, we are linking through our higher self to the realm of knowing (our instincts, intuition, inspirations, revelations, dreams, meditation). We start to develop the skills of being able to connect to the realm of knowing. When we learn about our own vision, we become inspired by it to a degree that we want to follow our own vision and fulfil it and so we become a vision-driven being. Upon becoming vision-driven, we start to gain a deeper knowledge of our own vision, know ourselves better at a much deeper level as we discover new abilities in ourselves that we didn't know existed before. As our newly discovered skills, abilities and knowledge become sharper and deeper, new feelings become known to us. By acquiring these new feelings, we start to:

- Rise,
- As we rise, we are further empowered by our own Life's Vision,
- We see better, and we will be able to see much clearer and wider than others around us as we rise higher, and higher, and higher.
- We start to perceive more while others may find it hard to perceive.
- Whilst in the past, we were just doing things absentmindedly, now we find that we can first see it in our mind before we do it, we act after we clearly see the result in our mind.
- We are focused on the needs of our vision, and we stop worrying about the little and petty things of life.
- We develop insights and wisdom as we are maturing along the way to fulfilling our Life's Vision.

- o We discover deeper insights about our vision by searching within.
- o We start meditating regularly and connecting with our inner voice and higher self, asking for advice and guidance.
- o We value our higher self by acting on the advice and insights we receive from it.
- o We regularly connect with our higher self for approval and guidance.
- o By following the advice of our own inner voice and higher self, we stop being influenced by others who disapprove of our dreams or vision for our life.
- o And above all, we will be working with the Rise of The Humans Framework to Rise even higher.

Rise of The Humans Framework

In Chapter 4, I introduce the Rise of the Humans Framework (ROTH Framework). The Framework compromises three Zones: the Red Zone, the Purple Zone, and the Green Zone. It also consists of the nine levels of rising as a human. As we work with the framework, we feel we are rising. Through the ROTH Framework, we deal with the issues that are bothering us in our life and in some way or the other the issues preventing and stopping us from discovering and fulfilling our Life's Vision. Issues that are similar in effect or like brakes which stop or slow down our progress. By dealing with these issues and adopting new values, we rise higher. As we deal with the issues in the Red Zone of the Framework, we remedy ourselves and balance our lives by discovering the values we lack in the Green Zone and becoming who we are based on the Purple Zone of the Framework. This process assists us in being lifted up and we start to feel that we are rising as human beings as we deal with these issues. In this process we learn to let our vision be World Embracing, The Rise of The Humans Framework (ROTH) assists us in the following ways:

The ROTH Framework helps us to let our vision embrace our family, rather than just embrace us. In the same way and at a different and higher level it assists us to let our vision embrace our community, rather than just embrace our family. Again, at a higher level, as we rise, it lets our vision embrace our city, rather than embrace only our community. As we rise higher, we let our vision to embrace our state rather than embrace our city only. Then, as we rise even higher, we let our vision embrace our country rather than just embrace our state. And finally, at the climax of rising as a human, we let our vision to embrace the world, rather than just embrace only our country.

At the end we become our vision

This book is about becoming. It is about how we can become who we are? Who are we born to become? Who we are here in this life to become, is the most important success you can ever imagine achieving in this life? This book leads us to the philosophy of being and becoming. It enables us to search our innermost and deepest realities. We will discover ourselves in a new way that we have never experienced before in our life. It portrays the true life of ours ahead of time for our preferred future, as a powerful guidance written by us, followed by ourselves, and achieved by ourselves. We do not need the help of anyone but ourselves as we read this book. Thus, we learn to become our own vision, and beyond that to become the guru of our Life's Vision.

The point is that we are here to make our mark in this world, the size of the mark is irrelevant. This book is all about helping us determine what our life vision is, helping us become certain of our vision, which makes us unique and significant, and helping us make our mark in this world. The vision that drives us to the fulfilment, is within us and the way to discover it, and fulfil it, is provided in an easy manner for an effective and efficient implementation.

The true nature of humans is revealed throughout the pages of this book and most people have not come across information like this, as this is unheard of before in terms of the knowledge and wisdom we gain. We may approach life the way that we were taught by our families and the environment we live in, unaware of the true philosophy of existence which as human beings is different from that of the animals.

This book reveals to us the secret of being human and guides us to access our true essence by finding our true Life's Vision within. By discovering our vision within, it becomes possible for us to get on the vision-driven path and start our journey of fulfilment and the achievement of success.

Everyone is destined to materialize something amazing, unique, and significant based on their Life's Vision that had not been materialized before his or her existence. He or she is the only one who has the key to unlock this gift and is here in this life to fulfil that. This means our vision is about bringing into existence something that never existed before, which we can cause to come into existence and is our contribution to our own fulfilment. It is like having your own child. Who else but you can conceive and bring into existence your own child, no-one, but you? In other words, the success of every human being depends on finding their vision, conceiving it and fulfilling it. Without fulfilling our vision, we are not done in this life and on this planet. The real achievement in our life is the fulfilment of our unique vision.

"The Law of Attraction" may be true but is not a guarantee of your fulfilment. "The Secret" may be true but will not guarantee your success. This is because, as you will discover, success is to find your unique vision within and then rearrange your life, re-plan your life, reorganize your life to fulfil that unique vision. As you do so, you will naturally attract and uncover more secrets that they discussed in "The Secret". Although "secrets" are helpful, they are not the assurance for success. The question is how do we define success?

The answer is that our success is defined deep down within us and is directly linked to our own vision. We may call it the Law of vision. The law of vision says, "your vision is buried deep down within you'. Our success in this life is based on finding it, conceiving it, and fulfilling it, this will lead us to our own success, and not a success that was planned or created by someone else. A vision that is defined by someone else is not our vision. Each person's vision is different from that of the others and is defined by the person himself/herself. We need to discover it and fulfil it. That is our success. The way others have defined vision and success is based on wealth and fame. Our vision and our success may include something that others have defined. Our success must not be defined by the level of wealth and fame but by the level of fulfilment of our vision. This is because it is the fulfilment of our vision that brings about wealth and fame. While wealth and fame cannot bring about our vision. It does not work the other way around. The point is that this wealth and fame creation does not work the other way. Those with wealth and fame have pursued their vision and fulfilled it and the wealth and fame were the byproducts of their efforts in the pursuit of their vision. This does not work in reverse. It is not appropriate to follow wealth and fame outside of our vision unless we know how these activities are linked to our vision and we know it. There are many examples of millionaires, and even billionaires, who end up having an empty life, no matter how much they have, and some even wished to commit suicide despite having achieved the highest levels of wealth. These are examples of when wealth is created but not linked to a vision of something bigger than ourselves.

As we journey through this life while pursuing our Life's Vision, we gradually merge with our vision and finally we become one with our Life's Vision. This oneness is the cause of happiness, this oneness is the cause of abundance and prosperity, ecstasy and joy, wealth, and fame. While we are following our vision, we are gradually realizing that we are becoming one with our life' vision, and at the end, it is through our vision that we will find ourselves. This journey becomes a journey of self-discovery. This is the story of who we are, which at the end, becomes the story of who we have become.

All these "the secret" and "the law of attraction" and so forth are all words and until they are understood, then acted upon, they will not work practically for human beings. Learning and the application of learning is a complex process and until we are competent in using "the law of attraction", "the secret" or anything else, these are just a bunch of words we call knowledge. Well, knowledge is fine but remains knowledge and can't go further. Although we might be in awe of such fabulous and interesting knowledge, unfortunately it remains at that level and cannot go any further. People might say, I am delighted to hear it, to know it, etc. and there is nothing wrong with that. It is okay, this means they are in awe of that knowledge. However, it is the practicality of the knowledge that becomes a problem, not how awe-struck we are by it. The practicality of the knowledge needs skills and action, and the elaborate working of these skills, as a bridge to connect and integrate that knowledge into action is what has been missing all along. It is okay to say wow! This is great knowledge, referring to "the law of attraction" and "the secret". How we convert that amazing knowledge into amazing action is what has been missing.

To rise as humans is to become able to convert amazing knowledge into amazing action and this requires competence. In other words, you need to have competence to act on amazing knowledge and convert that knowledge into amazing action, and as you learn how to do this in this book you will realise that this is how to rise as a human.

The Double Heuristic Method (DHM) was designed to explain the practical aspect of how amazing knowledge can be converted into amazing action, to bring it to a practical level. By doing this, we are then better able to teach and help those who are interested. This is what has been missing, not just from "the secret" and "the law of attraction", but also from Neuro-Linguistic Programming (NLP) and many other amazing bodies of knowledge.

This process enables us to perceive ourselves and the world around us through the lens of our Life's Vision whilst converting our knowledge to action. It is an amazing journey of self-discovery and rising fulfilment as a human being. Our own vision, which we are now becoming, helps us to grow and develop fully in this life, to prepare us to enter the "World of Vision' that is coming next after this life.

Our vision gives us wings

From the time we were born and at the early stages of our lives, and for some of us into the middle years, we have been seeking to find out who we really are. We are looking for answers, without knowing that the answer to the question of "who am I?" lies within us. Gradually, as we live our lives, we start to discover that we are here to become. So, the answer to the question of why am I here in this life? is: You are here to become. Now you may ask a second question: What can I become? The answer is: Find your Life's Vision, then you will know. Where do I go to find it? The answer is to search within and read the rest of this book, because we become our own master via our vision and the answer to who we are is gradually changing into who we are here to become. The next question is how to become it. The answer is when you discover it, you then need to convert the knowledge about your vision into action to become who you are here to become.

However, when we search for the answer to discover who we truly are here to become, we may realise that in fact what we are searching for ends up being our Life's Vision. In other words, our Life's Vision is similar or is extremely close to who we are going to become. The answer to who we are becoming makes sense to us and we feel comfortable with it, and we feel that it is the same as who we think or feel we are, who is in fact waiting to be discovered by us. After we have learned about our vision in this life, we are ready to start transforming within the chrysalis of our Life's Vision, to become the vision butterfly to rise and be fulfilled to serve those around us which is called our purpose. By becoming who we are then we possess the power of the "butterfly effect'. It is by attaining this power that we are able to serve.

When we discover our Life's Vision we start to develop as a new individual, a new being. How? Our vision serves as a nurturing and protective chrysalis, i.e. as a nurturing environment within which we start to explore internally and start getting ready to be shaped by our talents, what we love to do and the values that are important to us. These are the components of vision. By exploring within and finding these components of vision and applying them in our lives we transform and, at the end, become who we are, i.e., our own vision. After the transformation we acquire the power of "The butterfly effect'.

By transforming and acquiring the butterfly effect, with the power emanating from our being, we become empowered to embrace the principle of oneness with our audience, with our clients, our customers, or our fans, thus we become so spiritually inspired that we can influence the world. In other words, by becoming one with them, we rise again, further, and higher as humans with the spirit of service.

Hence, that thing, which we now have come to understand as our Life's Vision, forms a cocoon, the chrysalis, protecting us and allowing us to transform. We start to see it as the source and protector of who we are becoming. Then, gradually, as we transform, we start to realise that we are becoming our Life's Vision. By discovering this fact, we jump in our own skin, and feel a thrill of who we really were before the discovery. Whilst we had a kind of feeling of it in the past, now we feel it in full force. Upon this transformation, we start to feel that it inspires us, and that we become something which we are always getting excited about. When we discover it, we notice and become aware that our vision is associated with, and relevant to, something that we love to do, and that we also have the talent to do it well, because it is one of our strengths. As we go through this process, we realise that we are rediscovering ourselves in life by finding our vision. In other words, we are discovering ourselves by discovering our Life's Vision. We start to feel that our Life's Vision lifts us up, again at times this thrilling feeling comes back and lifts us up again, into the heavens and up towards becoming. As we are getting closer to discovering our vision, we realise a warm feeling within us, it seems familiar to us, not a strange feeling but a good feeling. The good feeling of an awe-inspiring uplifting and unfolding process of discovery, a eureka moment, and a heuristic feeling of rising as a human comes upon us.

Then, gradually, after a short while, we realise that we need to somehow articulate our vision, that we strongly feel our vision within us. On this journey, we gradually realise the benefits of discovering it, and become very certain about it, and we feel like dedicating our life to it. When any of these feelings are within us, around us in our thoughts and feelings, we should know that it is nothing else but our vision.

- It is upon discovering our vision that we feel we are rising; this amazing feeling comes to us. As it comes to us, we start feeling that we are rising higher, we feel the urge to want to rise higher. The urge of rising starts to captivate us. We feel that we are rising and being lifted. We sense, "it is this uplifting feeling experience" that we love. It seems to lift us at every moment, every instance, when we think about our vision or do something along the vision driven path. As we reflect on it, as we do something to think about it, as we act to make it happen, as we are being inspired by it, and as we wonder about it, we feel we are empowered by the lifting power of our own vision.
- Whatever we do with our vision, we sooner or later realise that whatever we do in our life we like to do in relation to our vision, because it lifts us up. We feel we are rising and as we truly feel it, we feel the power of rising, we feel the uplifting power of our vision. Whatever we plan, set, do, and act on in the direction of our vision we feel the rising experience at the same time. We feel the upliftment. Until we gradually realise that it is, and has been, the cause of the Rise of the Humans.
- Through these experiences, our vision gives us the feeling of Rising, as we start to Rise higher, we soon discover that as we rise higher, we can also view the

world better from above and through our Life's Vision. As we discover this reciprocal effect, our vision becomes an intense source of inspiration, and it inspires us to rise even higher. We notice that this feeling of rising is so like the feeling of having wings, like birds. We come to this realisation that our vision gives us wings. We realise that anytime we like to rise we can, by doing something and moving in the direction of our vision that gives us wings, living with the feeling of having wings gives us a special sense of the endless feelings of rising higher and higher. The uplifting feeling that our vision gives us brings us a limitless joy and we understand three significant points in our lives:

- The significance of connecting to our higher self
- The significance of finding our Life's Vision
- The significance of rising higher and the feeling of having acquired wings by merging with our vision and our becoming

These three points of significance are the reasons that lift us up and empower us, as humans, to rise above because of something we become that is bigger than us, we rise higher and higher. As we merge with our vision of becoming, we start to rise, rise further, and rise more as humans, there is no limit as to how much we are going to rise. We realise that we don't want anything but to continue rising and merging with our vision, we want only for our vision and ourselves to unite through to fulfilment.

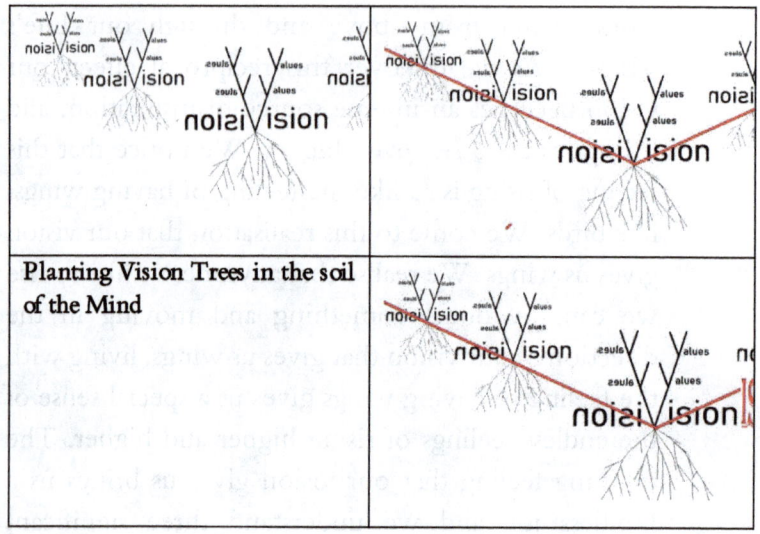

Figure 1.2 – Planting Vision Trees

Chapter 2
The Promise

Chapter 2 starts with the story of my mother in the last two years of her life and ends with looking at our Life's Vision and seeing how strong or loud it is. She was an exemplary mother. The chapter shows how I became a carer for her after she had a heart attack and needed care 24 hours a day and, how I cared for her in those last two years of her life. With tears in her eyes she shared with me her shocking story about her Life's Vision which transformed me. She often shared her regrets about her Life's Vision that went unfulfilled. I heard her stories about how important her Life's Vision was. She thought the circumstances in her life caused her to delay and further delay her vision until she lost the momentum, and she ended up with regrets. She asked me if I could do something so this never happens to anyone else. She said "This is the worst type of regret that brings pain to your heart when you realise there is not much time left and that you are at the end of your life". For this reason, I decided to write a book to prevent the pain of regret and clear trace of regret if it is already showing up in your life. This book is the panacea for the pain of regrets.

At her funeral, we released monarch butterflies as the coffin was being lowered. it reminded me to fulfil her wish. I promised her soul that I would create an approach and encourage people not to put their dream and vision on hold, but instead fulfil it within their lifetime.

During the two years I spent nursing her, she taught me many things and told me many stories about her life. While telling me those stories, she expressed on many occasions how regretful she was about not being able to become a doctor. She had always wanted to serve people in that capacity. She said that was what she would have loved to do, and she had always wanted to be a gynaecologist. After she returning home from the hospital, she revealed a secret that moved me. It also woke me up to the reality of our lives, which happened that night after the storm subsided. I noticed her gaze was locked on the television screen that night. I became curious about what she was watching as I noticed she seemed to have a great interest in the program.

I was silent pondering in my mind, "this was her Life's Vision", to be a gynaecological surgeon at the operating table, who can operate to deliver babies. Once again, she talked about her regret of not being able to fulfil her Life's Vision because of various unexpected circumstances in her life.

On another occasion, whilst my mother talked about regrets, she told me about human beings' success and regret dualism. At a different time, she re-told me what she would have loved to do in her career. With tears in her eyes, she told me how the circumstances of her life did not allow her to realise her Life's Vision, and how she was carrying the burden of her regrets because of her unfulfilled dreams. From the moment I understood, I promised her and myself to find a way to help others, so that no one will ever have to put their Life's Vision on hold and fall into the trap of regrets but instead rise to the heights of fulfilment as a human being before it becomes too late.

Society has defined success based on wealth and fame and forgotten about the individual's talent and Life's Vision that needs to be fulfilled. My mother asked me to do anything I could, anything in my ability to help everyone that crosses my path and anyone I can reach who needs help. She asked me to share her story as a lesson to all: "Never let anyone put their Life's Vision on hold". I promised her that I would write a book to share the story, to assist everyone in finding their Life's Vision and never letting anyone put their Life's Vision on hold, but instead to help people draw a plan to fulfil their Life's Vision and dreams.

In the world, we see some models for success that are based on wealth and fame creation. If it aligns with our Life's Vision, nothing is wrong with that. If not, then it won't work to create fulfilment, as these two feed of each other. The success of a few in creating wealth has influenced many others to pursue wealth and fame, but disregards one of the principles of best practice to becoming wealthy and famous, which is to follow your talents and do what you love in congruence with your values and your Life's Vision. So, this has created a situation in which many people subscribe to the wrong model or approach. If we pursue the wrong model of success, we may end up disappointed. Only by discovering and pursuing our Life's Vision we can achieve personal satisfaction, success, fulfilment that, in turn, can lead to wealth, fame and happiness.

Hence, the sole duty of everyone in this life is to discover their Life's Vision. If we have a dream, we need to articulate it and ask our higher self whether this is in congruence with our Life's Vision or in some way assisting our Life's Vision and our chosen direction. If not, forget about it immediately or as soon as we are able to, and we need to find something instead that is in congruence with our Life's Vision. Dreams are to be aligned with our Life's Vision; otherwise, those dreams will be unfulfilling.

There is an old saying I agree with which states that "Mothers are creatures of sacrifice." They sacrifice their time. They wake up in the middle of night to check on us when we are young, to ensure we sleep in peace and comfort. They make many sacrifices for us from our early childhood. Our mothers have these qualities and follow on their journey of motherhood with their unconditional love and care. We cannot reimburse their sacrifice if we decide to do so because we are unable to put a price on their love and sacrifice.

This is why we are all connected to each other as humans. I feel connected to you as the reader through our mothers. Sometimes their sacrifices are such that they do not pursue their Life's Vision. However, on the other hand, they prefer that their children follow their own vision. When it comes to matters of love, there is no right or wrong. However, I wished my mother could have pursued her Life's Vision from childhood. I know you feel the same about your mum too. My mother told me that she was helping the family in wartime. For months she carried buckets of water from the basement to the house above and helped with the cooking to feed her siblings. Hence there was no chance that her father could have supported her studies in medicine to become a surgeon or midwife.

Later in life, when she married at the early age of fifteen, she kept her vision alive, but "on hold' just as a dream and was always thinking of her dream of becoming a surgeon or midwife, but the circumstances of the family life did not allow for her to pursue her dream. As we cherish and love our mothers, we feel in our hearts their love, the love that made them sacrifice their ambitions and forgo their dreams to make us succeed, to support us in following our dreams and visions. As the Persian proverb says, "Heaven is under the feet of Mothers". A mother's love is the only connection our heart understands as true and pure unconditional love. It is a selfless love that our mothers gave to us in our childhood. Suppose we feel connected through the pure acts of love of our mothers that makes us stay connected and feel for each other as humans, with this connection. I think with this connection we can change the world. With this connection we can rise as humans and realise our dreams and Life's Vision.

From this point of selfless love and unconditional love we are connected as humans, it is divine, it is pure, it is sublime. This connection makes us human, bond as humans, survive as humans, love each other as humans, and prosper as humans because the power of that love, which is the mother of all loves, keeps us aflame all the days of our lives. From this point of love I am writing this book, inviting you to join me to celebrate this love together, a love that empowers us to discover and realise our Life's Vision. This is where we become one, we become one through this love and the love of our Life's Vision. The reality is we all have the feeling of such love that connects us all. We are all connected through this love as humans. No other love is above this love and by this love we are truly connected as humans.

She passed away peacefully with no pain, no movement though she was in deep sleep. I could see her face through my tears when she passed away. They moved her body to a particular room that is for people who pass away. She was asleep, calm, and peaceful. All the pains, difficulties, and sufferings were gone. She was so sweetly beautiful at peace.

I remembered her words echoing in my head. Since my mother passed away, her words kept echoing in my head, in fact in my entire body… "Homi, never let anyone get the point of regret, regretting that they did not follow their vision. It is the most painful regret, when the vision which you are the only one who can fulfil, based on your uniqueness, is left unfulfilled. It is painful for us, a loss for humanity and those we love.

Tell everyone to find their vision and purpose for their lives and fulfil it before they end up at the point of regret, as this is the most painful regret. Until someone has gone through it they may take it lightly. Believe me Homi, never let this happen to your children or anyone you know. If you can take it further to the world, please do. Promise me."

While tears were forming in my eyes, promised her that I would do that, and then I decided to write a book to take her message to the world as my own Life's Vision. When I was writing these lines tears were forming in my eyes.

Since then, I have dedicated my life, after her death, to this cause. This cause is to help those who do not want to put their Life's Vision on hold, and people who do not want to end up with regrets. I knew that there was an urgency to act for this cause. I recognised that this was the cause. The cause of helping people who need help.

Hence, for this cause a new approach was needed. I realised that by finding a new approach and a new way, we could serve this cause.

The Promise

I also realised that the approach must aim to help those who do not want to live a life where their Life's Vision has been put on hold by someone else, or by themselves. Rather they want to be freed from that bondage, want to live a free life, where they can freely follow their dreams, discover their visions, and take the journey of fulfilling their Life's Vision. This is an approach that helps them to discover and nurture their vision to prosperity and fulfilment, an approach that illustrates a way of life in which they are able to rise as humans, not to be put on hold. This is how the story of the Rise of the Humans began.

A few months had passed since her funeral and one day my gut feeling was urging me to go for a walk in nature. I normally respond positively to my hunches, so I decided to walk in the local Japanese Garden to reflect once more as I walk in nature.

I saw a Monarch butterfly in the park, so beautiful and gorgeous, one of those butterflies I released at my mother's funeral. I felt her presence and those memories came back. The memories returned. That day I was so emotional; my mother had passed away just a few short months ago. The memories of nursing her for two years during my busy life. I decided to chase the butterfly, hoping it would lead me somewhere in the park to see flowers, or plants. I noticed that every time I get closer to the butterfly, it flew a bit further. As I was chasing this butterfly and walking in the park, my memories of her returned and I felt the tears running down my face. She always told me how she missed the opportunities to follow her Life's Vision. I remembered one of those days when there were a number of beautiful white clouds across the blue sky. She told me to look at those clouds; as beautiful as they are, they must get to a certain height to fulfil their vision of making rain. When the conditions are right, and the clouds are at the appropriate height, the rain starts, the time to fulfil their vision. I said that I agreed with that analogy. To me, that height is similar to when we find what we love; and what our talent is, and it is also similar to discovering the most important values in our lives while searching within for our vision. I was reflecting on all these memories while walking and keeping an eye on that pretty butterfly flying in the park.

I recalled memories of how at her funeral we released so many beautiful monarch butterflies. So, each time I saw butterflies, I remembered her. As I chased that beautiful butterfly, I ended up near the lake in the middle of the park. The perfume of the flowers filled the air like a sweet-scented cologne. The ducks were floating on the lake as the yellowish ducklings played upside down. This park is part of the university and is used for growing various species of plant life. I continued my chase with the butterfly. I was walking amongst the trees thinking deeply about how best to write the book I was about to begin. I was sure I would write a book on Life's Vision, as I had promised my mother. The butterfly sat on a beautiful astounding gorgeous orange colour flower with verdant green leaves around it. My mother's soul, I thought, might be watching me wherever I go. I thought that I would dedicate the book to her.

The butterfly flew up in the air over the lake, as I was chasing it with my eyes. As the butterfly was fading into the sky over the lake, I heard birds chirping in the trees filling the air. It was calming and tranquil. The trees' reflection on the lake's glittering water was astounding. The trees were dancing on the water with the chirping melody of the birds in the background whilst little lights sparkling on the water's surface.

These glittering little waves reminded me of the box of diamonds my daughter showed me a few days ago. She used artificial diamonds to create home jewellery. As I was somewhat lost wondering about the beauty of the natural surroundings, my eyes caught a glimpse of a figure sitting on a bench.

As I was walking, approaching the bench where he was sitting, I said, "Hi, hello, such a beautiful day". The man who had a friendly smile and was wearing a hat, turned his face towards me. I noticed he had a beard; it was brownish, white, and greyish but charming. I thought his eyes had a special brown colour. I normally look into people's eyes to identify the ones interested in further conversation. He was one of them. I thought to myself, "his eyes were telling me that." He looked very friendly with a glow on his face.

He said, "yes, it is a wonderful day. This was exactly what I was thinking,"

I replied with a smile asking, 'How could you read my mind?'

He returned my smile with a smile too, "It is because we are all connected".

I said, "Fascinating, yes, I agree."

He mentioned, "Actually, I feel that way all the time".

I stretched my hand out saying, "My name is Homi."

He shook my hand and said, "Dr. Competence"

I had strange feeling that I was meeting myself. I felt strongly that this person was me, whom I have met. Although some people have experienced similar events like this, I realised it might sound like the strangest thing, but it was a genuine feeling.

It seemed like two sides of the same coin. Because I felt I was meeting the other side of the coin, myself, and I listened to him as if listening to myself, in my own voice. This was an amazing experience. I trusted him as I trusted myself and he revealed the answers to the questions that readers might have.

At that moment I realized this fact in my life; my job going forward into the future would be firstly to find the dots, and secondly to start to connect the dots.

Wow! that made me jump inside my skin. I remembered what my mother's spirit told me. In my mind, I saw my mother's spirit saying, "You will find someone who will help you without too much effort on your side". "But when you hear him, you must know something true; you have discovered the one who knows the answers to all your questions. So, you need to listen to him responsibly".

I did not know that I could find him so quickly. I thought it was astonishing and remembered what my mother told me about it. However, it seemed so unbelievable to me because I remembered the butterflies we released at mum's funeral, and a butterfly appeared here in the park and led me to this lake where I met Dr. Competence. I asked myself, "Is this a coincidence?" I was pondering the situation, not being sure of what to say, when I suddenly said, 'It is interesting to know there is someone by this name, nice to meet you." but not knowing why this was his name, I asked:

The Promise

Homi: How come you have such a title?

Dr. Competence: Do you mean 'Dr. Competence'?

Homi: 'Yes, Dr. Competence'

Dr. Competence: Because I have been researching on this topic, 'Competence', about 15 years.

Homi: Can I call you by your title?

Dr. Competence: Yes, you can.

Homi: What was on your mind when you saw me?

Dr. Competence: Okay, when you came, I was thinking about my childhood dream and vision in grade 9 in high school about my story of life.

Homi: Can you share it with me, I would like to hear it.

Dr. Competence: Okay, I will take you to the scene; where I went to school that day.

I found myself playing basketball on the school basketball court.

> *A breeze was blowing, touching my hair, while my eyes were fixed on the moving ball approaching me. With a sudden movement, I jumped up and grabbed hold of the ball, running with a dribble towards the post, and in my mind, the net was where the ball in my hand was going to land. I knew it. Suddenly, I saw Raz in the crowd. He was my friend. I aimed at the goal, throwing the ball, it went through. I made a fist holding my hand up in a gesture of success. I heard the crowd shouting and roaring and cheering.*

After the game I met Raz. He asked me whether I was ready for the Essay Class. I said I liked the teacher Mr. Yaghma. While talking to Raz in the schoolyard after the game, the bell rang, calling us for the start of another day of schooling.

We entered the classroom; the children were noisy as usual, but Mr. Yaghma was quite a serious teacher. We called him Mr. Y. Whenever his image was seen at the door, the room was silenced by his appearance.

Mr. Y entered the classroom, and silence ruled the air. All the students stood up, following him with their eyes, while he moved to sit behind his desk.

Mr. Y: Sit down

There was complete silence, Raz, sitting next to me, whispered in my ear, "Have you ruled your notebook?" I said, yes, I have. We had to rule the pages of our notebook, drawing a rectangle at the foot of each page with six spaces to write our name, class number and date. It had to be precisely on the correct spot on the page, as instructed, otherwise we were in trouble. Raz whispered, "my ruling is a bit wacky; I am scared."

Mr. Y: Put your notebooks in front of you, opening the page for today; I hope everyone has ruled their book as usual.

Class: Yes Sir

While it was silent, Mr. Y walked around the class to see if we had ruled our books properly.

"The theme for today is Vision of knowledge and vision of wealth for the future". He explored the progress of science, which has saved countless lives, together with wealth which has also saved lives, and explained that although both knowledge and wealth are great, they can also be used constructively or destructively." At the end, he said: "Fine, the title for today's essay is "vision of Knowledge or vision of Wealth" which one has a preference and why? Maximum two pages; start now, and remember, always follow your own vision and not someone else's. If you don't, you may end up with regrets."

The story started that day, and I wrote the essay on the preference of knowledge. My reason was, that we can achieve wealth with a wealth of knowledge. Hence knowledge has preference over wealth and can lead to wealth.

After the class, while we were walking out Raz told me he had thought of something. I said tell me, is it interesting? He said yes; and "I will tell you when you come to my place on Friday after school". I said, "Are you serious, Friday after school to go to your place?" He said: his mum and dad would not be home and would come back late so please come around! I will explain what I want to show you and my perspective on "destruction and construction" that day.

Homi: Such a fascinating story; thank you for sharing. Would you continue? I would like to know more, and it will be great to write about it too.

Dr. Competence: Maybe later: these were my thoughts before you arrived, now you tell me about your thoughts today.

Homi: My thoughts were about the book I want to write;

Dr. Competence: That is interesting: what is the genre?

Homi: It is a self-help book

Dr. Competence: Wow! interesting, great, tell me more. What is the main topic of your book?

I was silent, and I was lost in my thoughts when suddenly I heard Dr. Competence break the silence.

Dr. Competence: Are you with me? I asked what is your main topic?

Although I was lost in my thoughts for a few seconds, when I heard Dr. Competence voice, I was back with him.

Homi: The main topic or theme is 'Vision', as in "Life's Vision". What do you think about Life's Vision?

Dr. Competence, Usually, our life becomes our life as we live it, so we become clearer about how we would like to live our life by articulating our vision before we live it. This way, we will start to rise to the heights of fulfilment in our life.

Homi: Wow! That makes sense, but I have a problem fully getting it.

Dr. Competence: So, it is very wise, and important, to articulate our vision with competence to prevent regrets. It is the remedy for the prevention of life's regrets before it is too late.

Homi: And if we don't, what happens?

Dr. Competence: If we don't wake up to this fact, we may become part of someone else's vision, or we may end up with regrets and despair, as was said earlier. Do you remember Raz? He asked me to see him on Friday.

Homi: Yes, I remember what happened that Friday.

Dr. Competence: I was hesitant about going, but Raz reminded me again on that Friday Morning, so I decided to go with Raz to his home that day.

> *He asked me again, "Come with me today, I have a plan and I would like to share my view on "destruction and construction" with you".*
>
> *That day, we walked together to his house; it was a 15-minute walk to his house. When I compared this walk to the walk to my house, which was a 1-hour walk to school, I felt he was lucky to have a house closer to the school.*
>
> *We took a few shortcuts through the alleys until we stood in front of a three-story brick house with green curtains and large windows. There was a balcony in front of the second floor, and the rooftop was flat with a smaller sized room like a small cottage on that flat roof.*
>
> *He had the key and the door opened with a creak.*
>
> *We went through the front yard filled with tall trees and dark green bushy plants in between the trees. We were walking on a pathway, zig zagging until we arrived at an archway to a door.*

Raz looked through his bunch of keys to find the right one. The noise of the shuffling keys filled my ears. How many keys do you have? I wondered playfully. Quite a lot. Sure, enough, Raz found the right key and with a couple of twists the door opened. We entered a big hall, like a lounge room with a big beige sofa and chairs, a wooden dark brown coffee table and quite a number of lamps with shades. I was amazed by the number I had seen.

He said, "Don't touch anything, just follow me upstairs". We took a staircase, turning left midway, and up again to the second floor. We entered a corridor that seemed long to me and contained the doors to several rooms, all of which were closed. He stopped and reached for his keys again, for the third time, and opened the room. He said, "This is my room. Do you like it?"

The room had a long desk with two chairs, a bed, and a number of pictures in big frames. The curtain was green, thick, and closed. He turned the lights on and asked me to sit.

Would you like a drink? I have a small fridge with some milk, and orange juice, and cola. I said I would like a Pepsi. He said sorry, only Coca Cola. I accepted, and then he fetched the bottle and while pouring the coca for us, he said that he was excited to show me where he lived to me.

Afterwards, he showed me a collection of stamping pads, which I was used to calling "stamps that work like seals". These were made of rubber.

The Promise

Why do you have so many stamps? I asked Raz. He said he liked stamps. The reason I called you was to show you these stamps and to talk you into a plan. He was thinking of executing the plan at school. I was curious about what plan he wanted to share with me. He said we could become a band, and our goal would be to communicate in our own way. He said we could create a new stamp for our band and stamp a number of warnings to the class. I said we could use a small piece of paper, write our message, stamp each piece of paper, and drop them into everyone's desk early in the morning before the class started.

We designed the warning, "Be careful with your stuff, you will lose something if you don't."

We found a wine bottle cap that had a dragon carved in it. When we inked it and stamped it, we got a great seal to stamp under each of the papers. We then used a typewriter and made thirty notes with our seal underneath. Raz kept the notes in his drawer desk at home to bring them to school half an hour earlier than usual. I left his place after that meeting and went home.

As planned, I was at school earlier on Monday and met with Raz. How are you? Have you got the warnings? He said yes and we went to the classroom to leave the notes inside all the desks. We waited to see what would happen.

When a few students began to find the notes, they were a bit concerned and soon it seemed like everyone was talking about the warning notes. A couple of students even told Raz and me about the notes. We said we were aware of them too. The news eventually broke and reached the principal, and he came to our class right after the Bell Rang:

The Principal Said:

This note is not from the Principal's office or any of the teachers. We suspect it is from one of the students. As these notes were found only in your class, we think the suspect is also there.

At this point, students started turning around to look at other students. Raz and I looked around too, we saw each other, and I felt my heart racing.

As Mr. Y's words echoed in my head "Always follow your own vision and not someone else's; if you do you may end up with regrets", I thought to myself, "this is the last time I will follow someone else's vision or plan. I knew my vision was to become a teacher like Mr. Y and use my knowledge to teach the world. I knew in my heart that a time would come, sometime in the future, when the path to achieving this is clear to me.

Homi: Yes, I agree with you. In fact I lost my mother just recently, and she told me how regretful she was about not pursuing her own vision, but rather pursuing the vision of others.

Dr. Competence: I am sorry to hear that, but your mother was at the 'Point of Regret'

Homi: Point of Regret? What do you mean?

Dr. Competence: Sooner or later, every one of us will reach a point in our lives when we realise that our life is over and there is no way we can avoid our end.

Homi: Do we have time to review our decisions? Can we change anything?

Dr. Competence: By the time we realise that it is too late to change our past decisions, we may end up in regrets.

Homi: Can we guess or predict the point of regret, and make necessary changes early enough to prevent it?

Dr. Competence: Unfortunately, we cannot accurately guess the timing of the point of regret as it could come suddenly after an accident when we are older.

Homi: Ok, then what is our life best course of action?

Dr. Competence: The best course of action is discovering and fulfilling our Life's Vision, while we are healthy and have time, before old age and regrets kick in. There are many examples of elderly people who have expressed their regrets that you may have heard of.

Homi: Yes, I have heard of an Australian geriatric nurse who had been working with older people and collated a list of top regrets that these elderly people expressed.

Dr. Competence:
Yes, I know the story you mean, and I have read the book that she has written.

Dr. Competence explained more about the author and the book as follows.

The book is entitled "Regrets of the Dying" by Bronnie Ware. This book researched the topmost regrets most people have when they reach the point of regret.

When questioned about any regrets they had or anything they would do differently, common themes surfaced again and again. Here are the most common five:

1. I wish I'd had the courage to live a life true to myself, not the life others expected of me.
2. I wish I hadn't worked so hard.
3. I wish I'd had the courage to express my feelings
4. I wish I had stayed in touch with my friends
5. I wish that I had let myself be happier.

The first one, i.e. "I wish I'd had the courage to live a life true to myself, not the life others expected of me' has been the most common regret.

Bronnie researched and this is what she discovered:

> "This was the most common regret of all. When people realise their life is almost over and look back clearly on it, it is easy to see how many dreams have gone unfulfilled.'

> "Most people had not honoured even a half of their dreams and had to die knowing that it was due to choices they had made, or not made'. Bronnie Ware

Bronnie refers to an important point at which they know that it was due to choices they had made or not made. Bronnie was employed as a "Palliative Carer". She heard the regrets of patients' near-death experiences. The top deathbed regrets she heard during her time as a palliative carer were listed before. This is how Bronnie described her experience:

> "For many years I worked in palliative care. My patients were those who had gone home to die. Some incredibly special times were shared. I was with them for the last three to twelve weeks of their lives."

> "People grow a lot when they are faced with their own mortality. I learnt never to underestimate someone's capacity for growth. Some changes were phenomenal. Each experienced a variety of emotions, as expected, denial, fear, anger, remorse, more denial and eventually acceptance. Every single patient found their peace before they departed though, every one of them."

What regret means is that we have been incongruent with our vision or in our life. And that is why we feel regret. If we have some idea about what our Life's Vision is and feel regrets. It is because we are in disparity with our Life's Vision. We are, thus, able to bring our existing regrets to a resolution by aligning our decisions in congruence with our vision. If you regret past decisions, you need to know that you have been at variance with your Life's Vision, and have been incongruent with your Life's Vision or direction. If so, then move to resolve the regret based on finding out why you were at variance with your Life's Vision, and how incongruent you were at the time of your decision to resolve the regret.

The point is that as you have realised, it is not only your mother who had regrets; most people feel that way, as we can see by the listing of the number one regret as feeling despair at not pursuing their dreams or Life's Vision and this is in line with what Erik Erikson, the German psychologist emphasised.

At this point I said: I have heard his name. Is it true that he was a psychologist who moved to America later in life? He was one of the pupils of German psychologist Sigmund Freud and is famous for his 8 stages of psychological development.

Dr. Competence: Yes, we go through 8 psychological stages. Each stage leads to others and the last one is called Late Adulthood, which if not properly fulfilled, leaves us with regrets at the end of our lives.

From birth to when we are 18 months, we always need our parents' help, and we develop trust in our parents as well as the world around us; this is the first stage, called Infancy Stage. In the next stage, the Toddler Stage, up to 3 years, we start to develop independence to be able to walk and use the toilet, independently of our parents, and to do this, we need their encouragement and support.

If we do not develop good toilet habits, it may affect our self-esteem. The Preschool stage (3-6 years) is where we balance our curiosity and initiative, mostly mimicking others.

In the next stage, the school stage, 6-13 years of age, we need to be inventive. If we feel inadequate or have difficulty going through this stage, we may have self-esteem issues through the following stages. The adolescence stage (13-18 years). At this stage, we enjoy finding and discovering our identity. In the young adult stage, we are figuring out about our relationship with our partners and friends. In the Middle Age Adult stage, we are concerned about what Erikson called "Generativity", which means concern about others. In the Older Adult stage, we are concerned about "All Mankind' or an audience larger than others around us. While in the Young Adult stage we struggle with intimacy, in the Middle Adult stage, we are concerned with our personal development and the biggest fear is feeling meaningless in our lives. At the final stage, Late Adulthood, we either feel accomplished or, if we don't feel that, we feel Despair and a sense of not feeling fulfilled kicks in. In other words, the regrets kick in. Hence, Bronnie's findings confirm Erikson's findings.

Homi: How loud does our vision need to be?

Dr. Competence: Dr. Demartini emphasizes that "When the voice and the **vision** on the inside are more profound and clearer and louder than all opinions on the outside, you've begun to master your life".

Homi: Do you mean when it is loud enough, it will awaken the Giant of Vision within us?

Dr. Competence: When your Giant of Vision is awakened, you are on our way to fulfilling your Life's Vision with passion and enthusiasm, the likes of which you have never experienced before.

So, the answer to the question of how loud the voice and the vision on the inside must be is to the extent that it awakens your Giant of Vision.

Homi: Most people wonder when you ask them questions such as what is your Life's Vision? Are you certain about your Life's Vision? Do you know what we mean by "vision' in the context of our life?

Dr. Competence: Yes, I agree, however, some people say, "no, I do not know precisely what my Life's Vision is. I have not thought about that", or "no, I don't have one", or "I am not certain of what that means".

Homi: Life sometimes seems difficult, and it is not easy to find our way through life without a definite Life's Vision.

Dr. Competence: As we navigate our lives, we need a compass. Sometimes we are searching for our talents or what we love to do; we may ask ourselves, "am I going in the right direction in my life?' Why am I not very happy with my life's direction? Sometimes we feel no matter how rich or poor we are, we feel something is missing and we wonder what that is.

Homi: On the other hand, we always want to do something in our lives that is beneficial to the people around us. We soon discover that we have no single focus, and our mind may be all over the place. Or, if we think we have a single focus we may not be happy at times, jumping from one pursuit to another and looking for direction.

Dr. Competence: We are unaware that we have an inner life vision, a Giant of Vision Within, and we are looking for it in all the wrong places. There was a man who lost a gold coin in the dark, one night, he started searching on the ground where there was light, under the light which was a little bit further.

As he was searching, a policeman passing by noticed and asked him, "Sir, what are you looking for?' The man answered, "I lost a gold coin'. The policeman asked, do you remember where you lost it? The man said "over there.' The policeman said why are you looking for it here?' The man replied, because here is light; it is very dark over there, and I can't see. The point of the story is that you need to look to find your Life's Vision, but also, you need some light to see it while you are searching. This book provides the light for you to find your "Giant of Vision" in the right place within yourself.

That day our conversation fascinated us so much that we decided to meet again at Dr. Competence's residence the following Wednesday to continue our conversation about Giant of Vision.

So, on Wednesday of the following week, I went to Dr. Competence's place to meet him. When I arrived at the entrance, I found myself in front of an elegantly curved wooden door. I was excited and spent a couple of minutes looking around. Then I knocked on the door.

Shortly afterwards, the door began to open, and I saw Dr. Competence standing in front of me.

Dr. Competence: Come in, welcome; how was the drive? Did you find it well?

Me: No problem, it was straightforward, you have a beautiful place.

Dr. Competence: Thank you, Great to see you.

As I entered a huge lounge; a bit further down was the kitchen on the left, and the dining room was right in front, leading to the glass door that opened to a curved balcony. Dr. Competence's house was between the rivers. The lounge of the building was a two-level lounge. When I counted, there were forty chairs; the table was also a two-level table. I have never seen anything like this before. The table is a long table continuing from the upper half of the Lounge to the Lower half of the lounge and as you come to the first step down to approach the lower half of the lounge, so does the table. We stepped down, and he said, "be careful; watch the steps." I saw "watch the step' signs on both sides of the dining room. The good thing was that it was only one short step. I suppose they designed it this way because the house was atop a hill.

I was amazed when I heard Dr. Competence had a dream before the House was built. In the dream, the Balcony of the house was a big curvy balcony but less than a semicircle. From the balcony, I could see the vast rivers joining. Right below, in the river, I saw the boats on the blue surface of the river. Astounding, stunning scenery, I have never experienced it before. He showed me the library at the back. It was fantastic and had a small spiral stairway to pick up the books from the higher shelves. This staircase was dark brown with a shiny polished finish on it. It looked very elegant to me.

He said his dream guided him and his wife to build the house. The terrace in front was like terraces I have seen in the beautiful Bahai Gardens in Haifa, Israel, amazing and beautiful. There was a bean-shaped pool in the backyard of the house with a beautiful fence around it, filled with crystal clear water, and a short distance from it was a beautiful garden full of fragrant flowers, green and nicely trimmed.

At the other side of the library was his desk and behind it was a window with a curtain that was opened on both sides, like the window was a face, and the curtains looked like the hair to the face. There was an electric kettle and a tea set that looked Chinese next to the window on the side.

The Promise

In the middle of the library was another table with chairs around it. They were elegant. On the table were a few books with a book left open. There was a white piece of paper and a pen. Through the window, I could see the river. I thought that it must be the same river I noticed at the front, with the sailing boat on it. It was beautiful and, in the distance, I could see two more boats. The rivers' banks were covered by green trees. It was too far to tell what type of trees they were, but they were covered in green. There were also a few birds flying over those trees in the sky. The water in the river was a kind of greenish blue. I was thinking how lucky Dr. Competence is to live in such a house.

I said, "It Is amazing that you had a dream about this house.

"How do you do that?" I asked. He said he is a man of dreams, and it is true. I know this because later on that day, he showed me his book of dreams, where he wrote his dreams. On top of the book of dreams was printed, "Once I had a dream". On the cover was an image of a few footprints in sand.

He opened the book and showed me a few of his dreams, well written by ball pen, dated and even the time of the dream, e.g., I had a dream on 15/2/2016 at 3:00 Am. And the dream was ….

We sat there while having tea in Dr. Competence's library. As I had another sip of my tea, I was thinking about the last time when I saw him in the park, I remembered to ask him about how his Giant of Vision was awakened, and I was waiting for his response.

Dr. Competence: Yes, I will share my story of what happened when the Giant of Vision was awakened in me, because that is when we gradually start to realise that something in us that inspires us.

I started to work as a tutor in 1993. It was before a new program called the Training Packages was about to be introduced in Vocational Education and Training. When I began working as a tutor, I learned that the curricula, built upon competency-based training (CBT), had been massively reformed. I was doing my best to understand what was happening. I was in the middle of my journey to understanding CBT, which was new to teachers. The teachers were lost regarding how to deliver their content in the new format. When I studied the structure of the new curricula, I liked it. I knew the time had come for my Life's Vision to take shape, as something was happening to make my vision come true. First of all, I was now a teacher and secondly, I was able to creating something that could help everyone globally. Therefore, I spent considerable time to analyse the new format to master it while people around me were saying I was wasting my time. They were saying by the time you master it, it will change again.

In one of these conversations, I mentioned to the department director that I had resolved and simplified the complexity of the new curricula in a series of diagrams. I shared my series of diagrams with him. He showed interest and asked me whether I would be willing to show my diagrams to him in his office. I agreed to it.

During my illustration, he rose from his chair on several occasions and went to the whiteboard on the wall and redrew the diagrams. That day he confirmed my diagrams work. At the end of the meeting, he asked for a copy of the diagrams to share with the college director. I made a copy of my diagrams and explanations for him. A few days later, as I was walking through the college's corridors to go to my office, the Department director approached me and, while tapping on my shoulder, he told me, *"I shared your illustrations with the college director, and he was very impressed with your explanations"*. He also asked for a copy of your diagrams. I would like to thank you for your clarifying diagrams.

Sometime later, the college management decided to undertake a project to write six learning guides for the new curricula. Then, the teachers were invited to write a number of books. I undertook to write a book on Information Systems. Writing such a book required a new design that suited the new curriculum to be discussed in the writer's meetings as a work in progress.

At that meeting, I presented a new diagram based on my vision and proposed that the diagram be incorporated into the books. I argued that the diagram represented all the necessary components of the curriculum.

Teachers who could not understand the new model of the curriculum were disregarding it in their writing with some exceptions. They spoke in opposition to the change. The arguments gradually turned into a noisy debate and teachers were yelling and shouting in opposition.

No one knew that the College director was making coffee in the next room. Suddenly the door opened, and the director entered the room asking. *"What is going on and why are you having such a loud argument? What is the matter?"*

The teachers said, "Homi has presented a diagram and is arguing that it represents the units of competency, while we are arguing it does not."

The college director asked me, *"give it to me, let me have a look"*. Then he took the diagram. Everyone was silent while the director examined the diagram. After a few short moments he broke the silence by going to the whiteboard to draw a horizontal version of the diagram on the board. The screeching sound of the chalk on the board filled the room as teachers fixed their gaze on his drawing.

Then he said, *"This illustration is correct. Although he has illustrated it in a vertical presentation, I have drawn the same diagram in a horizontal manner."*

This incident awakened in me the Giant of Vision, especially when one of my colleagues told me, "Y*our interest in competence training and illustrating such complexity in a diagram is excellent. Why don't you undertake a PhD study in the area? You are already Dr. Competence!"* This signature story gave me the impetus to undertake further studies in this area of competence. I loved it so much; in fact, I became known as Dr. Competence later as a result. These events led me to create a new approach called the Double Heuristic Method (DHM), an approach to the teaching of competence, globally.

Homi: Wow, such an amazing story. So, your Life's Vision was awakened making you know who you were, and you got excited about yourself and your vision of becoming Dr. Competence.

Dr. Competence: Of course, and in fact we realise that we are getting excited about what our Life's Vision can accomplish for others and for the world.

Homi: And when we have this excitement, what happens then?

Dr. Competence: Then, we feel so great about ourselves as we realise that the Giant of Vision within us is urging us to move, to articulate our Life's Vision.

Homi: Do you mean we feel so strongly because of our Giant of Vision within?

Dr. Competence: Yes, we have the strong feeling that we finally want to become who we are at that stage in our life. And we become aware of the Giant of Vision standing inside us, and we feel we want to dedicate our lives to our Giant so that Giant of Vision finally becomes us. We become that Giant by discovering our Life's Vision.

Homi: Do you think that famous people are those who unconsciously or consciously their Giant of Vision? Do they know they have discovered a treasure of unlimited value, like the Alibaba story (because our Life's Vision is our real treasure!)?

Dr. Competence: Exactly, it is a treasure.

Homi: How do we see the world around us when we become our Life's Vision?

Dr. Competence: We start the journey of who we are and see ourselves and the world around us through the eye of our Giant of Vision.

Homi: Can you give me some examples I can understand clearly?

Dr. Competence: Yes, of course; an example was Gandhi: Gandhi's vision was the liberation of India and Indians. He and his vision became one. In other words, he finally became that vision, and through the eye of his Giant of Vision he saw the world, and he is now in the world of vision.

Homi: What do you mean?

Dr. Competence: Now, whenever we remember Gandhi, we identify him and know him by his vision because he discovered his vision, fulfilled it and became the Giant of Vision among his people and one with his vision. In other words, Gandhi found his Life's Vision, he pursued his Life's Vision, he became his Life's Vision.

Homi: Are there other examples?

Dr. Competence: There are many examples. Another example is Nelson Mandela. He is identified with the Apartheid in South Africa. He found his vision, pursued his vision, became one with his vision, became the Giant of his vision, and now he will be remembered with his vision.

Homi: what do you want to say in conclusion?

Dr. Competence: In conclusion, I can say, when we have developed the skills of seeing ourselves and the world around us through the lens of the eye of our Giant of our Vision, then, we become ready to enter into *'The World of Vision'* *like Gandhi, Nelson Mandela, Steve Jobs, Helen Keller, and many others.*

Homi: If we have difficulty finding our Life's Vision, where do you suggest we look?

Dr. Competence: Now that you know what is meant by Life's Vision and you want to know how to find yours. The short answer is you need to turn a number of stones to find the answer.

Homi: What stones should we look under first?

Dr. Competence: When searching for something, you need to be able to turn some stones over. The first three stones that you need to turn over are your talents stone, your love stone and your values stone. These are covered in the following chapters.

Homi: You mentioned Gandhi's vision; it is so inspiring to learn about Gandhi.

Dr. Competence: Yes, we are inspired by others' Life's Vision such as Gandhi, Martin Luther King Jr., Steve Jobs and Nelson Mandela.

Homi: Yes, I agree, they inspire me all the time.

Dr. Competence: Erikson wrote a book on Gandhi titled, "Gandhi's Truth".

Homi: What did Erikson say about him?

Dr. Competence: In the "Origins of Militant non-violence', Erikson, talking of Gandhi, says that he used non-violent strategies.

Homi: Did he set and achieve some goals congruent with his vision?

Dr. Competence: Definitely, all his goals were in congruence with his Life's Vision. In order for his Life's Vision to be fulfilled, he set a number of goals within those strategies, using his values.

Homi: What about Martin Luther King?

Dr. Competence: Martin Luther King, Jr. was different regarding the country he was living in, with racial prejudice.

Homi: He also had a vision which he communicated in his famous speech, "I have a Dream"

Dr. Competence: His vision was a world free of prejudice so that people with white and black coloured skin could live in harmony. He used a special focus on non-violence strategies. His strategy was delivered through non-violence demonstrations.

Homi: What about Steve Jobs?

Dr. Competence: Well, Steve job's Life's vision and how he fulfilled it was also very significant?

Homi: What were his goals, strategies, values, and focus?

Dr. Competence: But we can start by covering Gandhi and his vision?

Homi: That is fine; Gandhi had a formidable personality, didn't he?

Dr. Competence: Yes, indeed, his personality and character were so formidable that Einstein sent letters to Gandhi because Einstein and Gandhi were contemporaries and communicated with each other.

Homi: What did they communicate about?

Dr. Competence: They exchanged a number of letters.

Homi: What did Einstein think of Gandhi?

Dr. Competence: He mentioned that "We may all be happy and grateful that destiny gifted us with such an enlightened contemporary, a role model for generations to come."

Homi: This is a touching, meaningful, and uplifting comment about Gandhi by Einstein.

Dr. Competence: His Life's Vision became clear to him. It was to free India or to achieve India's independence.

Homi: What were Gandhi's goals and achievements?

Dr. Competence: There were several goals. Some writers and researchers have listed about ten or more goals that Gandhi achieved in South Africa, and in India, in the course of freeing India from British rule, leading to India's independence.

Homi: Can you name a few of these goals?

Dr. Competence: For example, when Gandhi arrived in the Champaran District of India, he realised that the farmers were receiving almost nothing for their work, as landlords were in control; also farmers were heavily taxed by the British.

Homi: How did he reverse this?

Dr. Competence: Gandhi used his strategy of non-violence to achieve his goal, and he led some protests against the landlords controlling the farmers and paying them nearly nothing. This resulted in landlords signing agreements to reduce their control and pay higher and fairer prices for the farmers' produce. This was a great achievement for Gandhi.

Homi: What were his major achievements

Dr. Competence: He achieved two important and significant goals that led to independence.

Homi: What were these goals?

Dr. Competence: The goals were, the Salt Walk and the Quit India Movement goals.

Homi: Yes, I have heard about the Salt March. How is it related to the "Quit India Movement"?

Dr. Competence: Well, in the Salt March, his goal was to uphold the legitimacy of India's independence.

Homi: How did he achieve his goal?

Dr. Competence: As the British Salt Act deprived Indian people of the right to produce salt in India and came with heavy penalties for those found in breach, he decided to walk 388 kilometers (241 miles) to Dandi to reach the sea and produce salt from the sea.

Homi: And then what happened?

Dr. Competence: Gradually when he started the walk, thousands of people joined him for this walk. The Salt was produced despite the Salt laws and the news was reported extensively by various media. Many were arrested and jailed for Salt Offenses. The world started to realise that the Indian claim for Independence is legitimate. However, about 80,000 Indians were arrested in the process.

Homi: What did this victory lead to?

Dr. Competence: He started a Campaign that was called Quit India Movement that demanded the end of British Rule in India. Massive protests started all over India following his Quit India speech.

Homi: I also heard that thousands of people were arrested again.

Dr. Competence: About 100,000 were arrested, but this led to the announcement by the British Government that after World War II, the Power of Government would be transferred to India. The 100,000 who were prisoners were released. His life inspired Martin Luther King Jr. and Nelson Mandela.

Homi: What were Gandhi's attributes and qualities, or even better, his values? What were the values he upheld in his life?

Dr. Competence: He had many values that he adhered to as part of his personality. His values were, Non-violence, Honesty, Bravery, Humility, Love, Truthfulness, Take the first step and Live in the present. Gandhi said, "An eye for an eye makes the whole world blind."

Homi: What was his main message or vision to the world?

Dr. Competence: When they asked him, what is your message? He said, "my life is my message." That is why I have always said our vision is our life. Ultimately, our Message becomes our life, or our vision becomes our life.

Homi: Do you think his focus was on the idea that "My life is my message"?

Dr. Competence: Yes, that is a reasonable assumption to make, given all the facts.

Homi: What do you think his strategies were?

Dr. Competence: We can conclude, from his life, that his strategies were resistance by non-violence means, organizing peaceful demonstrations, walking, speech, hunger and abstinence from food.

Homi: What was his knowledge? How much did he know?

Dr. Competence: He had knowledge of Indian culture and the Indian system of government. He also had knowledge of the law.

Homi: Now, considering all these bits and pieces of facts, how is it possible to present them in a summarized fashion?

Dr. Competence: We can achieve this in a Tree of Vision.

Homi: In this case, what does a Tree of Vision for Gandhi look like?

Dr. Competence: Based on all the bits and pieces of data we have gathered about Gandhi's vision, his Tree of Vision may be depicted as follows:

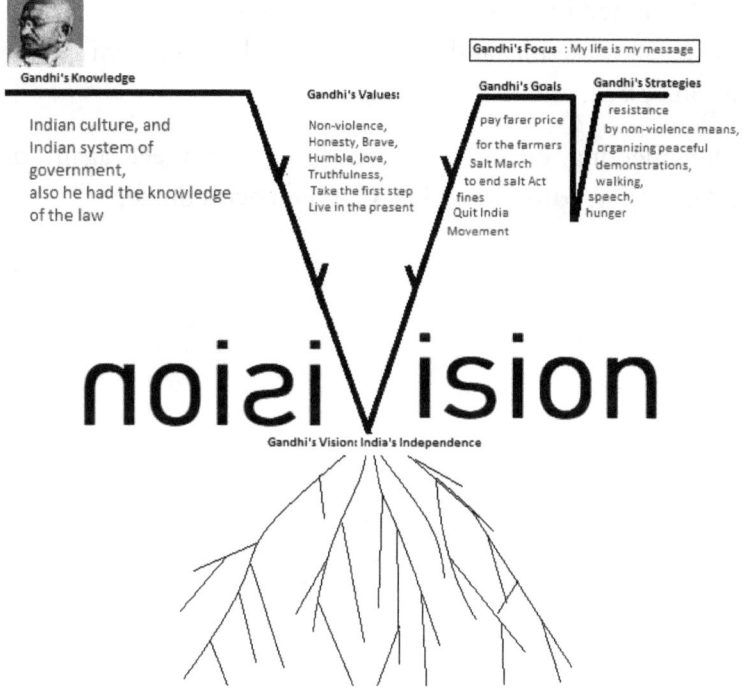

Figure 2.1 – Gandhi's Vision Tree

Homi: This is interesting. Similarly, can we create the Tree of Vision for example for other visionaries such as Steve Jobs, Nelson Mandela, and Martin Luther King?

Dr. Competence: Of course, we need to collect all the details and bits of data to create their Trees of Vision.

Homi: What is a Tree of Vision good for?

Dr. Competence: It summarizes how someone has fulfilled his Life's Vision. In Gandhi's case, it illustrates how many goals he achieved, what strategies he used for the achievement of his goals, what values underpinned his goals, what knowledge underpinned his actions, and what his focus was. It is possible to see all these bits and pieces of data about Gandhi's vision in one place, and it is awe-inspiring.

Our meeting ended, and we agreed to meet again the following Wednesday at Dr. Competence's office.

Chapter 3
Our talents and what we love.

*"You have something you are good at, and **you are gifted in that way**. If you do not know your talents and your gifts, you go in different directions endlessly in your life." – Unknown*

Today I met Dr. Competence in his office, during his lunch break as we had arranged before. When I arrived at the university where he works, he was waiting for me in the canteen. It was a huge canteen. He told me that there is a huge dining area and after that, there is a nice area with tables and chairs, and some sofas for teachers and lecturers at the end of the canteen on the right side of the coffee shop within the canteen. When I arrived there it was almost 12 noon. I crossed the huge dining area where the students gather and sit to have lunch. The murmuring sounds of the crowded place filled my ears with the wind of the kind of buzz you may hear in noisy places. It was even difficult to hear someone speaking in that noise. At two corners of the dining room on the left side where I was walking through, there were some crawling plants on the walls and some of them were growing to the ceiling, creating the illusion of hanging off the ceiling with quite a prolific growth of green leaves covering parts of the ceiling. The arrangement of tables and chairs was in diagonal rows of hundreds going in each direction; a huge place to dine, I thought to myself. The lighting fixtures were very long and provided florescent light to the place via hundreds of framed fluorescent lighting units in the ceiling. As I approached the teacher's area, I noticed some more mature people sitting to have their meals in a more spacious section that looked more comfortable. I could see Dr. Competence sitting in that area of the canteen before he noticed me. As I approached, he began to stand up for a greeting, but I asked him to please sit. He stood and said that he was having a drink, while waiting for me to arrive to get lunch. He said follow me and started walking towards a large food counter next to a coffee shop. We went to that counter together as we chatted.

Homi: You know I was thinking about talents, and what we love, and I concluded that our talents are what we receive from our genes.

Dr. Competence: I agree with the point that our talents are innate.

Homi: Do you also agree that we are naturally gifted by our talents?

Dr. Competence: Everyone has certain innate talents. Our talents gradually become evident during our lives. We have some idea of what our talents are. Everyone is good at doing something; and as stated above **"you are gifted in that way"**.

Homi: Do you also think that if we do not discover our talents and gifts, we may go in different directions endlessly?

Dr. Competence: Of Course, as we become clear about our talents, we want to nurture them.

Homi: But how much of a role can our talents play in our Life's Vision? Can our talents guide us to our Life's Vision?

Our talents and what we love.

Dr. Competence: Some may think that way. We also need to nurture our talents.

Homi: On the other hand, Goethe stated, "we are shaped and fashioned by what we love'. Does it mean that what we love also shapes and fashions our Life's Vision?

Dr. Competence: We are going to explore what difference they make as we go through our discussion and discover what the answers are.

Homi: So, we will explore both sides of this coin, the coin of talent and love, are we? Because as Carl Jung says, "we look into our hearts, where the love is, we are awakened."

Dr. Competence: Yes, true, and we can start this understanding with a quote from Steve Jobs. He delineated that:

"The only way to do great work is to love what you do. If you haven't found it yet, keep looking, don't settle. As with all matters of the heart, you will know when you find it." - Steve Jobs

Dr. Competence: Now, what Steve Jobs is highlighting is that we do what we love, and the opposite is also true, that we love what we do. So, the time has come for you to find someone who has discovered his/her inner talents, and as you write the book, involve him or her in the process. Does Steve Jobs' reference to "Matters of the Heart' remind you of someone you know who has found what they love to do?

Homi: The "matters of the Heart' that Steve Job is talking about firstly reminds me of you, and secondly of Lilly.

Dr. Competence: Lilly? You never told me about Lilly? Who is she and how do you think her story relates to the "Matters of the Heart" story that Steve Jobs mentioned?

Homi: Well, I prefer to listen to your story before I tell you Lilly's story.

Dr. Competence: Are you sure?

Homi: I am certain.

Dr. Competence: Okay, I told you the story of Raz in my childhood. I also told you the story up to the point when my colleagues encouraged me to do further research on competence.

Homi: Yes, I remember, what happened then.

Dr. Competence: Then I applied to do a research study on the Topic of Competence.

Homi: Which university did you apply to?

Dr. Competence: this was a university called, Central Queensland University. I applied to study how simulation can be used to develop Competence. That was when I started. The memories of Childhood once again came to me. If you remember, I told you that the article I wrote in Grade 9 was still with me and that I needed to have my own theories and knowledge. So, I became very excited about the study as I remembered Mr. Y, my teacher when I was in grade 9.

Homi: Were you accepted? What happened to your application for the study? Did you hear from the University?

Dr. Competence: Yes, I received a letter, and I was admitted to the Course.

Our talents and what we love.

Homi: Was it exciting?

Dr. Competence: I was on top of the world, so excited, and this was a dream come true for me.

Homi: What happened after that?

Dr. Competence: I will tell the rest later. Now let me know the story of Lilly.

Homi: Lilly's story is breathtaking. I met with Lilly the day after we arrived in China. She came to our place wearing a new costume or uniform. I was so excited to see her. After we hugged her, my daughter jumped on her affectionately and embraced her. My daughter calls her Mummy Lilly.

Dr. Competence: Mummy Lilly, that is interesting. So, your daughter calls your wife Mum, and calls her Mummy Lilly.

Homi: Yes, that is true; her name is Lilly. She is always full of enthusiasm. She spoke about Tai Chi with absolute excitement and enthusiasm and told us that we needed to see her new studio which she had opened. This was her facility/business venue for teaching, practising, and learning Tai Chi.

Dr. Competence: So, then?

Homi: We eagerly listened, as she what she loves to do and that she has the talent to do it well.

Dr. Competence: How fascinating.

Homi: Yes, it is, and as I was thinking about writing a book on Life's Vision and fulfilment, I was carefully listening to what she was talking about. I became fascinated by her enthusiasm and excitement because I was looking for anything that could help me write the book I was thinking of writing.

Dr. Competence: That is so fascinating to me, and I want to hear more about it. Please tell me what happened after that.

Homi: After that she was telling us how it took her some time to discover what she loves (to do) and that now she has discovered it. She said she has a teacher, who is the master, and that her teacher is guiding her to be the teacher she aspires to become. I thought her first Studio for Tai Chi was excellent and she had spent so much time and energy to getting it started and that now everything is happening for her. We had Dinner together that night. When she was leaving, she asked me I could visit her in her Tai Chi studio the next day at 9 AM.

Dr. Competence: Did you go?

Homi: The next day, I woke up and, after breakfast, got ready and left to find the place. I walked down the street to the crossing at the traffic lights. As I was crossing, I noticed the shops were interesting in this area; some were noodle shops that open early in the morning, some were shops selling household items, and some were selling items made of straw. Our place is in Daxu Gujen, an old traditional city in Guilin, the Gunashi Province in China. I turned right from the traffic lights and walked for some distance then turned left into an alley lane, crossed the bicycle lane, turned left again, and found myself in front of the studio.

Dr. Competence: How was Lilly's Tai Chi Studio?

Homi: It was great; the high ceiling was the first thing that caught my attention. There was also a huge poster when I

Our talents and what we love.

entered the hall in front of me but across the opposite side of the entrance door. It was a photograph of her teacher in a white Tai Chi outfit. He was performing a Tai Chi move, similar to familiar martial arts gestures, holding his hands up in a certain way that Tai Chi practitioners and martial artists do. There was also a huge mirror on the right-hand side of the big studio on the wall where I could see myself full-size when performing Tai Chi movements. It is very useful because you can see how you look in case you need to correct your posture, so whilst performing, we can look in the mirror and ensure we are moving in the right manner.

There were a few people there and Lilly was there. She introduced them to me. Some men and some ladies were in the studio that day, ready to start performing. It was about 9:20 AM. They told me that they were starting to practice Tai Chi in a few minutes at 9:30 AM.

Dr. Competence: What else did you notice?

Homi: On the left side of the Hall, in the Tai Chi studio, was a long table where I could see some Chinese calligraphy brushes, pens and paper.

Dr. Competence: So, tell me about Tai Chi; how did you find Tai Chi?

Homi: Well, at 9:30 AM that day, one of the students stood in front of the mirror, facing the mirror. The rest of us lined up behind him on both sides. We stood in a position where we could see him and have a good view of ourselves in the mirror. I found out that his name was Mr. Wang. The first thing he did was the Tai Chi stance. He stood still, looking into the mirror, right and left feet on the ground about one foot apart, to create a stable stance. Next, whilst holding both hands outstretched, we learned to make a fist, with the four fingers of both hands formed into a fist and the thumbs in an up gesture. With that posture, we had to stand like a statue for 15 minutes without moving. This is called the Tai Chi stance, with our feet about one foot apart.

Dr. Competence: What is this good for?

Homi: It is good for stability.

Dr. Competence: What happened when the 15 minutes were over?

Homi: Lilly joined us, and we followed Mr. Wang and Lilly to perform more Tai Chi moves. The eight moves for warm up, then Tai Chi stance on one leg and Tai Chi walk.

Dr. Competence: How many moves are in Tai Chi

Homi: As Lilly told me, there are 74 moves in Tai Chi, and of course, as a beginner, we learn the eight moves first. When the exercises finished, it was about 11 AM. I stayed a few more minutes to have a cup of tea. I left the Tai Chi Studio and went back home.

Dr. Competence: How many days did you continue to do Tai Chi?

Homi: I was doing Tai Chi at least three times a week at that time.

Dr. Competence: What happened next?

Homi: Lilly came to our place again. She brought a white Tai Chi uniform for me.

Dr. Competence: Did you go to Tai Chi Studio again?

Our talents and what we love.

Homi: Yes, in fact, the next day, wearing the Tai Chi uniform, I went to her Tai Chi studio, and I was amazed. After we had done the Tai Chi stances, moves, and walks, Lilly asked me to sit and watch the Tai Chi fan and sword show. Then all the Tai Chi ladies got together in colourful uniforms and with a big red fan, (those hand-held Chinese fans) they started to perform Tai Chi Moves with the fan which was so fascinating that I felt as though I had been to one of the big dance performance halls. This was amazing as every move was combined with hand gestures whilst holding Chinese fans, producing an amazing visual effect. I recorded some of these Tai Chi moves with my mobile phone.

A sword dance followed this. It was a performance, similar to Tai Chi moves when the warriors use swords for defence. I videoed these as well.

During the week before I departed for Europe, I went to the Tai Chi studio as much as possible because I discovered that Tai Chi is great for maintaining our body's balance.

Dr. Competence: Where did you go after China?

Homi: I left China for Paris, France.

Dr. Competence: Why were you travelling to Europe?

Homi: It was all about the book I was thinking of writing on Life's Vision. I was scheduled to go to Greece to a city called Kalamata, where they grow olives.

Dr. Competence: Yes, I have heard about Kalamata, and the famous kalamata olives.

Homi: The Seminar I was going to was in Costa Navarino, a beautiful, picturesque part of Greece in the Kalamata region.

Dr. Competence: But you said you went to Paris instead; why?

Homi: Because my cousin's family in Paris, I took this opportunity to visit them before I headed to Greece.

Dr. Competence: Okay, did you see your cousin?

Homi: Oh yes, I did. Despite a cold October, I enjoyed visiting the Eiffel Tower.

Dr. Competence: Fantastic! So, what happened after Paris?

Homi: After Paris, I left for Greece via Amsterdam. After a one-night stay in Amsterdam, I flew to Kalamata. When I arrived, I found a small airport. I just came out of this small airport, talking to a couple of locals and found them very amusing and interesting. They were sitting on a bench smoking. The lady spoke English and said, we just visited Kalamata and we are going back to Athens. She was waving her hands because of the smoke her husband was puffing. "You do not like him smoking?" I asked. She said, "I was a smoker too, but when I heard the risks of smoking, I quit. But not him; he tried to quit many times, but he is smoking again; and telling me darling, don't worry, I will quit once more when we reach Athens. I was laughing and said maybe this time he would succeed. The husband said, "Don't worry; if I don't succeed, I will try again. I never give up trying to give up, and that is the secret of my success!"

Dr. Competence: How did you get to your hotel that day?

Homi: After that, I got a Taxi and went to my hotel at Costa Navarino.

Dr. Competence: What happened there?

Our talents and what we love.

Homi: Well, lots of good things happened. Two stand out for me.

Dr. Competence: What were they?

Homi: I meditated every night to come up with a book title that the publishers would accept as good, and this happened. The other discovery was to design a cover that makes sense for the title. These two were my achievements in relation to my Life's Vision.

Dr. Competence: Interesting; now tell me more about Lilly. What was she doing before she became interested in Tai Chi?

Homi: She had been a reporter and photographer but had yet to be sure that this was for her, and she recently discovered her Life's Vision is Tai Chi.

Dr. Competence: How passionate was she about Tai Chi?

Homi: Yes, she was eagerly passionate, enthusiastic, and excited about Tai Chi. She loved it exceptionally.

Dr. Competence: Are you in touch with her?

Homi: We communicate on WeChat. I asked her to send me the following lists to create the Tree of Vision for her teacher: A list of goals achieved, A list of values he has in his heart and an itemised list of his knowledge. What strategies have he planned to use to achieve his goals? and What has been his focus?

Dr. Competence: And what did she say?

Homi: She said she was in Nanjing. Her teacher is busy, holding a meeting. She highlighted that her teacher organises Tai Chi conferences. That her teacher is great, and she is weak.

Dr. Competence: What did you respond to her?

Homi: I said, "You can model him by looking and improving. To do that we can create his vision tree on paper. I said we needed that information particularly his values.

Dr. Competence: Why did you ask her for the information?

Homi: I will include this in the book, because we can all learn from Lilly's case.

Dr. Competence: How did you discover her, and how did you find out she is so interested? Her case is an exciting story to follow.

Homi: The story started when I decided to go to China as we had a quiet place away from everything to write the book. There, I met Lilly again. Although she had been a family friend for some time, this time when she realised that I was writing a book on Life's Vision, she showed some interest in learning more about it. Her determination and passion for what she had recently discovered were enormous.

Dr. Competence: What about her level of enthusiasm which you just mentioned?

Homi: I noticed her enthusiasm and passion for Tai Chi and that she wanted to model her teacher to improve and become who she is. She proved to be a candidate for inclusion in my book because she was in the early stages of vision planning with the new direction.

Dr. Competence: What was her reaction when you mentioned her inclusion in your book?

Homi: She was excited when discovered that I wanted to include her in the book. So, I decided to interview her on

Our talents and what we love.

the book's tenets, the vision-driven approach, and while working on the book, review her planning and her Life's Vision.

Dr. Competence: You can leave these masters of vision for later, and as I have a suggestion for Lilly.

Homi: And that is?

Dr. Competence: As Lilly is already following her teacher, who is her Tai Chi leader and master, you can do her teacher's Vision Tree and compare Lilly's Vision Tree with that.

Homi: Great Idea; I have already sent her a message requesting the components I will need to create her teacher's Tree of Vision.

Dr. Competence: This is great for Lilly, as well as others, who can learn from her example if they are going to model their hero, leader, or coach to improve.

Homi: This is a great plan

Dr. Competence: Let's do it

Homi: Ok, I am so happy.

Dr. Competence: For this plan, you needed to do two interviews, one with Lilly and one with her teacher.

Homi: As her teacher was always travelling and was very busy, I asked Lilly to provide me with the components of Knowledge, Values, Goals, Strategies and Focus to create her teacher's Tree of Vision.

Dr. Competence: Oh, excellent; what about Lilly herself?

Homi: Based on some guided questions, I interviewed Lilly to gain insight for the readers, as this education is missing in all the schools around the world.

Dr. Competence: What is interesting about her?

Homi: The exciting thing about her is that she is full of enthusiasm. Every time you see her or if she arrives in a group, she influences them and starts to make them move, make them excited and then in the next minute, she guides them to do Tai Chi. She leads with her movements, and then everyone follows her, going around the room and doing Tai Chi. Everyone is joyful.

Dr. Competence: She is a great candidate for what we are planning, and if she agrees to share how she is progressing, you can find out her Life's Vision and help her fulfil it while you are writing the book.

Homi: It sounds great.

Dr. Competence: This story is uplifting and shows how to become our Life's Vision; discover it, plan it, follow it, and fulfil it.

Homi: And I think I can add that whoever reads these materials will be able to take the wisdom and lessons learned and apply it to their lives, all the way through to fulfilment and feel that they are rising higher as they are working on something bigger than themselves, i.e. their Life's Vision. As Confucius advised, "the essence of knowledge is having it to use it" and competence is the application of our knowledge and skills to what we are doing in our lives.

Dr. Competence: Ok, on that basis, let's start composing Lilly's story.

Our talents and what we love.

Homi: Once upon a time, there was a girl called Lilly. She was always looking for and trying to identify her vision. She wanted to become a visionary and she knew she needed to find her Life's Vision. She tried many things/vocations but was not yet satisfied with what she was doing.

Dr. Competence: That is interesting; what happened to her before she was confident that she had found her Life's Vision.

Homi: She searched to find her Life's Vision. At first she wanted to become a reporter. She tried to learn the tricks of the trade, and finally to some extent she was progressing.

Dr. Competence: Was she sure that it was her Life's Vision?

Homi: No.

Dr. Competence: Was she looking to find something else as her Life's Vision?

Homi: Yes, Lilly confessed that, as she was searching, she realised her interest in calligraphy. During this time, she was in contact with teachers in China. As most teachers in China develop outstanding skills in calligraphy, she knew of many teachers that occasionally assemble.

So, she joined these large gatherings of teachers interested in calligraphy. From the large spectrum of people, she could see how they all approached the pursuit of their Life's Vision.

She did not feel fulfilled pursuing calligraphy, which she followed for some time. She concluded this was not her Life's Vision either.

Next, she learned about photography and thought that this might be her Life's Vision. In pursuit of photography, she gained knowledge and skills. She produced fantastic photos.

She was interested in travelling, so she travelled extensively to take photos of many beautiful sceneries in various parts of China.

As a result of being a photographer, she went to many different small towns, big cities, and various provinces, and spoken to various people and groups. She also got some teaching experience in calligraphy.

As she was interested in gaining knowledge of how other people find their direction in life she networked and came in contact with many businesses.

She said that she had seen many people who did not even think of finding their Life's Vision. Some might have given up or didn't bother. Some were exhausted from trying to find their dream. They were merely living which drained them of their energy. And they did not have the energy and enthusiasm to find their Life's Vision.

On the other hand, she saw many other people, who had discovered their calling, their direction, and their Life's Vision. They were successful, happy, and content.

People who had given up on finding their vision and were exhausted, about what kind of life they were having. Why they were unable to cope, and some were just doing mundane things such as eating and sleeping without any eagerness to follow their dreams or visions.

The other group were full of enthusiasm and excitement and happiness. They could not be in one place, and they wanted to be in touch with people with lots of jolliness and energy and were always on the move and excited about life.

Our talents and what we love.

When she enquired and spoke with these two groups, she discovered that those who were so excited and enthused about their lives were the people who had discovered something that the first group did not have. As a result of being a photographer when she enquired further to find out what it was.

She discovered that the second group who were happy and excited had found their Life's Vision. Something that they loved to do. Something that they enjoyed doing. They celebrated doing it, and they were fascinated by it.

Lilly decided to find her own Life's Vision from the moment of this discovery. A dream that was hers, and represented her to the world. She knew that when she could live her Life's Vision she could enjoy the same feelings that the second group of people enjoyed.

At that time, as part of her quest, she always asked people, what you do? Questions like, "Do you like your business?" Then she would pay attention to their answers. One day she met a businessman, and when she asked him her usual questions. His reply was: "Yes I like it, because it has always been something I wanted to do", and "finally, when I opened this business, I felt I had done what I should have done". The next question that Lilly asked him was, "Do you have a talent for what you do?" He said, "At the beginning it was a lot to learn but now I know everything, and I think I have the talent."

So, Lilly was asking them these questions, and she noticed that those who had found their Life's Vision seemed to have confident smiles as they answered her questions. She still did not quite know what her Life's Vision was. She still was not sure if the photography was her vision.

When I first met Lilly, she was in this massive house with her two dogs. The house was full of photographs. Hundreds of works of art, photography, and calligraphy covered all the big walls with high ceilings.

People visited this house to see the art and the calligraphy. This continued for quite some years and during that time she was still looking for something else that would be her Life's Vision, that she can share with China and the world.

As Steve Job advised: *"If you haven't found it yet, keep looking, don't settle. As with all matters of the heart, you will know when you find it." - Steve Jobs*

So, Lilly was still looking, and she hadn't settled, as our vision is a matter of the heart and as Steve advised us, we should not settle until we find it. This was precisely what Lilly was doing.

Since I visited her last time, I learned that the big photography hall had gone, and then I realised that she has now opened a Tai Chi studio.

My wife was a psychologist and a Bach flower therapist. She also had many patients who needed help with their calling. They needed to learn what their problem was. Some developed insomnia; some developed various health problems. Lilly was talking about who still needed to understand their vision. They did not know their Life's Vision, some had not even heard the significance of it.

Lilly checked with a number of people. Some were Day Dreamers, some were Goal Setters, some were Planners, and some were visionaries who believed in their visions.

The Day Dreamers were just talking about and wishing to be excellent in some way but not going further than that. Those

Our talents and what we love.

who were dreamers were referring to their dream and hoping it may come true one day.

The Goal Setters were individuals who just set goals and started to achieve them. They believed that we must have goals as human beings. When we have goals, of course, we need to achieve them, but most of them don't. After a short time, those who achieve their goals feel the same again, which means they feel like setting another goal. They believe that they must have goals as human beings.

The Planners are constantly planning for anything they want to do. People with a vision always plan and then set goals. They dream about their Life's Vision and bring it to fulfilment. They live in unity with their vision. Their goals are congruent with their vision, and their achievement has meaning. Their goals bring them closer to the fulfilment of their vision. It is all about a win-win living, it has such a profound meaning.

After speaking with these people, she realised that those who find their Life's Vision are those who succeed most of the time. Lilly discovered that there was a master of Tai Chi who was a teacher and ran a business in Tai Chi. She heard that this man is a Visionary. So, Lilly called to ask if she could make an appointment to meet him.

After the master agreed to the appointment with Lily and made a remarkable discovery. The teacher asked Lilly, "Do you love Tai Chi? Do you have the talent for Tai Chi?" In other words, the Master meant whether her skills supported her to become a Tai Chi instructor and teacher. The teacher told Lilly: We must explore ourselves and discover our talents. Everyone has specific innate talents.

Dr. Competence: Abdul Baha explained that. "Everyone has innate talents." Our talents gradually become evident during our lives. We have some idea of what our talents are. As we become clear about our talents, we like to nurture them.

Homi: But the question is how much can our talents play their roles in our vision – Can our talents become part and parcel of our vision?

Dr. Competence: We need to nurture our talents and bring our talent advantages into our Life's Vision.

Homi: As has been referred to and discussed, we come to this life with certain talents. We know what we love, our likes and dislikes, and the values we cherish in our hearts. We know that we are here to do something that we love.

De Competence: Because this is what Steve Jobs mentioned, that like other matters of the heart, we know we are exactly where we should be. Our Life's Vision is our personal cause which will fulfil that our essence deep down within ourselves knows.

Homi: And do we know why this is so?

Dr. Competence: The underlying reason is that our Life's Vision which is born of our talents, what we love, and the values we cherish in our hearts, becomes the most meaningful thing to do. When we have reached this level of meaningfulness, our entire being becomes aflame with empowerment and we become a source of inspiration and enlightenment.

Homi: You are right, and as Steve Jobs has mentioned, Lilly knew when she came up with the idea of the Tai Chi teacher. There was a sparkle in her eyes. It seemed that something

Our talents and what we love.

clicked inside her. And there she was. Something made sense, and she discovered it immediately. A sparkle of meaningfulness grabbed her and took hold of something inside her. It seemed that she was aflame.

Dr. Competence: Yes exactly, at whatever stage of life, you are at, once you discover your true Life's Vision, just pause, reflect, meditate, and make a decision to pursue it, because the sole reason you are in that point in time in your life is not an accident. This is because your life becomes so meaningful upon discovering your Life's Vision and you know it when this happens.

Homi: Such a brilliant and fascinating experience. How might people feel at that point? What a fantastic feeling it is. It is so beautiful and meaningful.

Dr. Competence: Because you discovered the reason for your existence, and nothing is more beautiful and meaningful than this in our entire life.

Homi: All of that is crucial and so beautiful and meaningful in this life.

Dr. Competence: You know Homi, the most profound meaning of our life is not what we have done but what we must become. And that is why its discovery enlightens us. It is the real enlightenment, The truth about us, which is as meaningful as it gets. There is no higher meaning in our life than this.

Homi: And when we understand and grasp this meaningfulness, what do we need to do, what is our next step?

Dr. Competence: Then, our next vital step is to fulfil our Life's Vision to become that enlightenment, that meaningfulness. That is why we are here and must do it. The fulfilment of that meaningfulness is the next thing to do.

Homi: So, if someone asks us, we would say that is why I am here, this is who I am, and therefore I am here to become?

Dr. Competence: And this is the best cream of our personal growth, no matter what we have done so far for our professional and personal development. Personal change happens when we interact, and this is the interaction with ourselves that brings out the best in us as we start exploring to discover and follow our vision of becoming.

Homi: For this meaningfulness and enlightenment of personal growth, do we need to go through a process of transformation, or does it just happen?

Dr. Competence: A transformation similar to what happens to a caterpillar in the chrysalis occurs after we grasp the meaningfulness.

Homi: Do you mean grasping this meaningfulness makes us ready for transformation?

Dr. Competence: Exactly! The stages of becoming, like a butterfly, which is a symbol of becoming, and gaining the power of flying nine. Nine is the largest one-digit number. It is the symbol of the highest level of growth we can achieve. Similarly, rising as a human being by our vision needs to be explained, through nine embraces. This process begins with enlightenment when we grasp this meaningfulness.

Our talents and what we love.

Homi: What happens after grasping this meaningfulness, before we rise, before we fly, and we are lifted up by our vision?

Dr. Competence: After this enlightenment and meaningfulness about our vision in this life, we are ready to transform within the chrysalis of our Life's Vision to become the human butterfly.

Homi: Can we then achieve our purpose?

Dr. Competence: Yes, by developing and attaining the spirit of service, the seventh stage of our transformation in the chrysalis of our vision, we can serve, and that is our purpose. It all happens after becoming.

Homi: Please explain a bit more clearly?

Dr. Competence: See, the caterpillar cannot fly before it becomes a butterfly, even though it had the vision to become a butterfly. When a caterpillar becomes a butterfly, it can serve the flowers. It must fulfil its purpose after. It cannot enjoy the benefits of being with flowers or pollinating them in advance. In other words, when it could not serve its purpose when it was a caterpillar.

Homi: Okay, I got the point. What powers do we acquire when we are becoming?

Dr. Competence: When we are becoming, we acquire the power of the butterfly effect. We have this new power, "the butterfly effect".

Homi: What is this new power and how can we use this new power?

Dr. Competence: Just imagine how many millions of lives can be impacted and changed by your Life's Vision. And the only time that we access the power of the butterfly effect is when we discover our vision and fulfil it. Understanding and utilizing the butterfly effect power of our Life's Vision we can impact millions of lives.

Homi: What does this transformation do for us?

Dr. Competence: When we discover the enlightenment and the meaningfulness of our Life's Vision, we start to transform through the nine embracing stages of becoming a new individual a new being.

Homi: How?

Dr. Competence: Our vision serves as a nurturing and protective Chrysalis, i.e., as a nurturing matrix or environment within which we start to transform internally. We start by exploring within to become ready to be shaped by our talents and what we love to do. We are supported and nurtured by the values that are important to us and that we cherish in our hearts.

Homi: What are these?

Dr. Competence: These are the components of vision. By finding these vision components and applying them in our lives, we start to transform within that matrix.

Homi: How do we discover more values in this process?

Dr. Competence: Our growth within that matrix of vision becomes evident by developing and nurturing these values in our hearts. While dealing with life's challenges which life throws at us, and by choosing to confront these challenges

Our talents and what we love.

we are led to use our heartfelt values or adopt new values in our life in pursuit of our vision.

Homi: How can we face these challenges?

Dr. Competence: By applying our existing values or developing new values we can nullify the effect of those challenges.

Homi: Can you provide some examples?

Dr. Competence: At the end of this transformation, we might acquire the power of butterfly effect.

Homi: What is the true meaning of "the butterfly effect"?

Dr. Competence: It means that a flap of a Butterfly's wings has the potential to create a tornado or storm sometimes later and somewhere else such as on the other side of the earth.

Homi: How did this come about?

Dr. Competence: Edward Lorenz was a Meteorologist. In 1961, Lorenz was using a computer on a numerical model for weather prediction. While he was entering data, he used a numerical value (0.506) instead of (0.506127). This small decimal fraction discrepancy (of 0.000127), in rounding his figures, resulted in a completely different weather scenario. He published his finding in a paper in 1963. Another meteorologist has commented that if Lorenz theory had been correct one flap of a bird like a sea gull's wing would affect the change of weather patterns for ever. This theory was known as the "The butterfly effect".

Homi: What can we learn from this, please sum up?

Dr. Competence: What we can learn is that, when we are transformed through this process, our vision has the potential to influence our lives, and the lives of millions of people around the world.

Homi: How does the butterfly effect work?

Dr. Competence: It works like this: if we drop a small rock in the pool the butterfly effect of it is that it produces bigger ripples as if we used a big rock. In other words, your vision can create more significant results than you imagine it would.

Homi: Can you provide some examples of the butterfly effect and Life's Vision?

Dr. Competence: In Gandhi's vision, every small action he took, like a small rock in the pool, created ten times, even a thousand times more ripples. Finally, these ripples resulted in a massive changes in India and worldwide. You can find more examples in history, even in recent times. They even say that the ripples of Gandhi's vision influenced Martin Luther King in the USA, and Nelson Mandela, in Africa. Even years after Gandhi, you can trace the effect of those ripples.

Homi: What can we learn from the butterfly effect?

Dr. Competence: When our vision has the butterfly effect, the ripples reach audiences more extensively than we thought. We feel empowered to embrace the principle of oneness with our customers, clientele, or the audience we serve. This ripple effect, together with the spirit of unity and oneness, is necessary for our vision, particularly for our business, if we have one.

Homi: Do you mean our business will benefit as a result?

Dr. Competence: Yes, when you adopt the spirit of service, one of the values you need to adopt is unity and oneness.

Our talents and what we love.

Oneness with your customers, clients, fans and audience. Customers will be inspired by the spirit of unity and oneness that they see in your organization and the services you provide. When they see that, they will remain your customer for as long as they feel that spirit of service and oneness. In personal life, your friends or those around you who are attracted by your vision will remain friends, customers, followers, or fans. At the same time, they feel unity and oneness.

Homi: Does this spirit of oneness makes us rise as humans?

Dr. Competence: Precisely, thus, we become so inspired that we can influence the world through the power of our vision, similar to the butterfly effect. In other words, by becoming one with them, we rise again further and higher as humans with the spirit of service.

Homi: What do you mean by further and higher?

Dr. Competence: I mean that by every move, we influence larger audiences than our audience, more extensive clientele than our clientele and customers. It implies the butterfly effect is working, and while it is working, we rise as we grow with our Life's Vision. And, with such a strong sense of growth, we advance on the vision-driven path. We will soon realise that we are getting the best of ourselves as we rise higher like an eagle.

Homi: Do you mean we are growing and rising higher with the butterfly effect at work?

Dr. Competence: Yes, we are developing and growing personally and contributing more through the power butterfly effect.

Homi: Okay, I think I'd like to change the subject now. You know Steve Jobs stated that, "As, with all matters of the heart, you will know when you find it." What does matters of the heart mean?

Dr. Competence: Steve Jobs is referring to the point that we need to search and search until we find something that we truly love to do. When it happens, like in Lilly's case, you will know it.

Homi: What do you think, are we better off when we follow our talents, or is it better to pursue what we love?

Dr. Competence: Goethe, the German poet says, "we are shaped and fashioned by what we love". To lead a vision-driven life is to allow ourselves to be shaped and fashioned by what we love.

Homi: Do we need to focus on what we love or what we don't love?

Dr. Competence: Both our likes and dislikes guide us to find our Life's Vision.

Homi: Do you mean we need to pay attention to the activities or things we like to be involved in, as well as what we do not like at all?

Dr. Competence: We know what makes us feel great and what things we run away from. In other words, what things are attractive to us, and what things distract us? Magnets attract bits and pieces of metal; they love metal pieces.

Homi: How can we find out about this great feeling, love?

Dr. Competence: We can explore to find out deep down, what it is that we love. Also, what is it that we love to do in

Our talents and what we love.

this life? Because that will shape us into vision-driven people and propel us to rise as human beings. All human beings can rise, and it is the time of, "the rise of the Humans".

Homi: Does it have the power to lift us to the heights of fulfilment?

Dr. Competence: Yes, I'll give you an example. Think of an orange tree. The orange tree loves to produce oranges and by doing it, it fulfils being an orange tree.

Homi: Do you mean that is a good metaphor for human thinking?

Dr. Competence: Yes, it is the same with us as humans. They say that everyone has been given an innate talent. We have that natural talent that serves what we love to do in this life.

Homi: How do we discover what our talents are?

Dr. Competence: Discovering and searching within to explore our skills and likes and what we are good at, sometimes we may need meditation to lead us to our talent.

Homi: When we are confident that we have found our talents and what we love to do, what do we need to do to pin down our vision? Do we need to discover anything else?

Dr. Competence: We are almost there when we know what we love and our talents. However, we also need to discover what our values are. Then, we are able to easily find our calling and vision after discovering these three items.

Homi: OK, what is the difference between our vision and our purpose?

Dr. Competence: Our vision is something to become. Like a butterfly, it is about becoming. Our purpose starts from when we have become. When we have fulfilled our vision, we can now do what we love to do to serve others and our community. We start doing what we love to do with the help of our talents.

Homi: From the time we discover our vision, to when our vision is fulfilled, where are we, while we are becoming? Are we on the vision-driven path?

Dr. Competence: While we are on the vision-driven path, we are in fact, within the chrysalis of our vision transforming to become like a butterfly. Our journey on the vision driven path is the journey of transformation into the Butterfly of becoming. Our Life's Vision is from where we are to the fulfilment of our dream.

Homi: What about goals? Should we set up some goals to achieve? How does that work?

Dr. Competence: Every goal that we set, becomes a stepping stone. These goals are about becoming and they are based on vision-driven aspirations, which move us forward in our plan of fulfilment. These goals are like stepping stones that pave the vision-driven path. By realising a vision-driven goal, we are one more step forward. During our vision-driven journey we may set several goals, as we achieve them, we transform.

Homi: What do you mean by "Vision-driven life"?

Dr. Competence: While we are in the process of transformation, we are living our life as a "Vision-driven life". We are engaged in this transformative life. Vision-driven life is a life in that every move is a vision-driven move.

Our talents and what we love.

Even every breath you take is a vision-driven breath. Every goal is a vision-driven goal. Every effort is a vision-driven effort. Every thought is a vision-driven thought. Every smile is a vision-driven smile. Every victory is a vision-driven victory. It is a life of transformation.

Homi: So exciting, engaging, fantastic, and heartwarming. I may have even run out of words to describe such a life. Beautiful.

Dr. Competence: Yes, it is. You cannot compare this life with any other form of life. You do not transform your life unless you live it as a vision driven life. You are transforming when you are living your life as a vision-driven life. While you are transforming the transformation is somehow invisible. However, you do not want to change it for any other type of life.

Homi: How do we feel living such a fantastic life of transformation?

Dr. Competence: When we live a vision-driven life of transformation, we feel peace and contentment. We are directed by our vision, and we are not lost. We feel a sense of confidence about ourselves that others may notice because we are rising. Also, we are very clear about what we are doing.

Homi: What do you mean by being clear, are we not?

Dr. Competence: Clarity is important. In this process, clarity removes any doubts that we may have. It gives us a sense of certainty and confidence, knowing where we are heading.

Homi: Is it all about a vision-driven life and the path we are travelling on?

Dr. Competence: Of course, it is because vision-driven goals are very clear, and should be. Our vision is clear, and it should be. Our transformation is clear, and it should be. That is why whoever is on the vision-driven path is very clear about what they are doing, as clear as pure crystal water.

Homi: Yes, for example Lilly told me she has set 10 clear vision-driven goals. She told me that her vision was like crystal water. Her vision-driven purpose is also clear as well, to become internationally known for Tai Chi. She wants to be known as the Tai Chi Angel.

Dr. Competence: What are her Vision-driven goals?

Homi: Her Vision-driven goals are very clear. She wants to train 10 Tai Chi teachers in China, in many provinces, and help them to open and manage ten Tai Chi centres and her goal is clear to attract new members to each of the Tai Chi Centres.

Dr. Competence: These goals are clear vision driven goals for Lilly's vision leading to her success.

Homi: Can you elaborate what success is or means?

Dr. Competence: What success means and what success is, are two different things.

Homi: What do you mean, by two different things, what are they?

Dr. Competence: Success is to discover your vision, your talents and what you love. Then plan and implement the plan to realise your dream by being on the Vision-driven path. It is about living a vision-driven life, utilising your talents.

Homi: Then what success means?

Dr. Competence: Like an orange, what orange is and what orange means are two different things. While the orange is a fruit (like what success is), it is different to what the orange means. For example, for some, it may mean orange colour. For others, it may mean vitamin C, and for a third person it may mean orange juice, orange marmalade, orange peel or part of a fruit salad.

Homi: Can you clarify by referring to the meaning of success?

Dr. Competence: In terms of meaning, success has different shades of meaning. It could mean the maturation of your talents. Success means your love of what you do expands and gives you more joy and excitement. It could mean discovering your values, that your transformation is happening smoothly on the vision-driven path. Success could mean excellent fulfilment of your vision. Success could mean being able to serve people and the community around you are enjoying your services. Success means the sense of satisfaction that you have achieved. Success could mean that you have been rising and lifted into the heavens as a human. Success may mean that you are now being lifted up. These are some of how success is meant. The process of staying successful on the vision driven path, to transform as you progress to realise your calling, your vision. And now you can sing the song, "O my vision, lift me up, lift me up, lift me up, lift me up into the heavens."

Part A - Finding Your Talent Activity

Activity – Please provide your top three answers to the each of questions in the following table.

Questions	1st Response	2nd Response	3rd Response
What you are good at?			
What things you like to do?			
What do you enjoy doing?			
Who do you cherish?			
What games do you play?			
What games do you watch?			
What sports do you watch?			
How are your abilities about music			
What kinds of Art do you love?			
What are your strengths?			
What are your talents?			

Our talents and what we love.

What skills have you developed that you are using?			
What hobbies do you have?			
What do you do in your spare time?			
What business do you have, or what type of work do you do?			
List the activities that you loved in the last 10 days? How much time did you spend on each activity?			

Table 3.1 – Heuristic Questions to discover your Talents

Part B - Discovering what you love to do Activity

Homi: Okay, with that in mind how do we go about our natural talents?

Dr. Competence: Steve Jobs referred to finding what we love to do in our life:

"The only way to do great work is to love what you do. If you haven't found it yet, keep looking, don't settle. As with all

matters of the heart, you will know when you find it." - Steve Jobs

Also, Goethe said that we are shaped and fashioned by what we love. So, think about what it is that can shape and fashion your life?

Homi: You are the one who knows deep down within you what you love that shapes and fashions your life.

Dr. Competence: We will be discovering what we love to do by being sincere and honest, in our enquiry.

Activity:

The purpose of this activity is to remind you about things you love, and one of the things that you love is what you love to do in your life? These questions will help you to find it. So, think about love, what you sincerely love to do that shapes your life and you absolutely love it. Please provide your top three answers to the questions in the following table.

Questions	1st Response	2nd Response	3rd Response
What do you care about?			
Does philanthropy excite you?			
What country would you love to live in?			
What do you love to do in your life?			

Our talents and what we love.

What movies do you love to watch?			
What job would you love to do?			
If you love to do business, what type of business do you love to do?			
What companies / businesses would you love to work for?			
What books have you read that you loved?			
What activities do you love to do?			
What do you love to do if you have time?			
What do you love to buy if you have the money for it?			
What pets do you love the most?			
What writers do you love?			

What actors do you love the most?			
Which singers / musicians do you love?			
What is the colour you love?			
What dress do you love to wear?			
What cars do you love to own or drive?			
Anything else that you love which is not listed?			

Table 3.2 – Heuristic questions to discover what you love to do in your life

Chapter 4
Rise of The Humans Framework (ROTH)

Let your vision embrace your family, it is better than if it just embraces you.

Let your vision embrace your community, it is better than if it just embraces your family.

Let your vision embrace your city, it is better than if it just embraces your community.

Let your vision embrace your state, it is better than if it just embraces your city.

Let your vision embrace your country, it is better than if it just embraces your State.

Let your vision embrace the world, it is better than if it just embraces your country.

Homi: How can we explain the understanding that the true seeker on the path of vision acquires while setting foot on the vision-driven path?

Dr. Competence: That is a good question to start with. Let's consider that a true seeker on the path of vision will grasp a profound understanding that every human being is governed and controlled by a set of values and attributes that he has adopted consciously or unconsciously throughout his life. And that he might be conscious or unconscious of these values, but these values have become part of his being and unconsciously are influencing his decisions, goal setting and goal achieving, even further, these values influence his actions and the fulfilment of his Life's Vision.

Homi: Okay, but what about if he has some issues from the past that influence him not to follow his vision?

Dr. Competence: Let us also consider that parallel to the above process, we occasionally reflect on some decisions and actions that we have taken in the past, judgments we have made, and circumstances we have gone through in our life as a result of which we have ended up with some issues and problems that we are struggling with now.

Homi: Should we dig into these issues and find out what caused them?

Dr. Competence: Well, no matter what has caused these issues and problems that may be disturbing, and what we might have in our lives, they need to be sorted out and cleared. In particular, if these issues are preventing us from pursuing our Life's Vision and the goals we are going to achieve, which in most cases they do.

Homi: What is the role that these issues play in our life?

Dr. Competence: These issues and problems guide us to the values we need to be added to our list of values. The point is, if we want to fulfil our Life's Vision genuinely, we need to these problems and issues to clear them.

Homi: Why?

Dr. Competence: Because not only do we need to eliminate the barriers preventing our progress in realising our dreams, fulfilling our Life's Vision, and achieving our goals, but also this process helps us to pin down the values we lack that are vital for our success.

Homi: Why do you think we are here in this life to find the values we lack?

Dr. Competence: I believe we are here in this life and on this earth to discover the values we lack and adopt and nurture them to pursue our Life's Vision.

Homi: True.

Dr. Competence: And it is through finding and fulfilling our Life's Vision that we grow.

Homi: How can we explain that?

Dr. Competence: The answer to how to explain it is this: We gain all the knowledge we are here to gain, learn the skills we are here to learn, achieve the goals we are here to achieve and focus on the way that we are here to focus, as well as using specific strategies that we are here to use to fulfil our Life's Vision.

Homi: And why do we do this?

Dr. Competence: And we do all these to experience our lives and to adopt, develop and nurture those values that we are here to develop, grow, improve, and perfect ourselves by.

Homi: Why do we need values?

Dr. Competence: Because by adopting the values that we lack, we can wash away our faults and improve the relationships around us. As we do so, we will find the profound meaning that our values play in our lives and the impact they have all along the way, throughout our lives.

Homi: What would be the result we get from this?

Dr. Competence: When we do this, a profound meaningfulness fills our souls with joy and happiness like we haven't experienced before.

Homi: How do we benefit from dealing with our issues?

Dr. Competence: These issues are guiding us to the values we lack. In other words, these issues are our guide to finding the missing values we need on the vision-driven path.

Homi: How many types of issues are you talking about here?

Dr. Competence: To succeed on our journey to fulfilment, we might be dealing with nine types of issues. These are explained in the nine stages of the Rise Of The Humans (ROTH) Framework. We need to go through these stages in order to rise as humans.

Homi: How does this happen, and how did you create the (ROTH) Framework?

Dr. Competence: In my research to construct the Framework, I have been inspired by the work of Baha'u'llah, AbdulBaha and Dr Bach. The result of my findings is presented and has been condensed into the Rise Of The Humans (ROTH) Framework. The story began with the revelation I received in my meditation of October 17, 2010, to connect with my Higher Self, to help individuals achieve love, light, and unity, in their family, community, and the world. I thought about this for quite some time over many years: How can I do something to make it possible for more people to achieve this love, light, and unity? I felt strongly that this must be possible through everyone's Life's Vision, because everyone is endowed with a vision to fulfil in their life, no matter how big or small, the fulfilment of it is what's essential, not its size. I knew that a Framework would be critical to bringing this into reality. This Framework will assist everyone who is willing to rise as a human in pursuing of their Life's Vision.

Homi: How did the works and writing of Baha'u'llah, AbdulBaha and Dr Bach lead to these findings? Can you elucidate further?

Dr. Competence: Of course. In the works of Baha'u'llah and Abdul-Baha, some references encourage humans to adopt and use positive values and virtues when facing negative traits. Also, Bahaullah emphasizes that we need to let our vision be world-embracing. These references in their works inspired me to research the creation of a Framework for the Rise of the Humans. I thought, I had two final stages constructing the Framework. I was looking for some inspiration to complete my work. While searching, I came across the work of Dr Bach, which had some similarities with the work of Bahaullah and Abdul-Baha in terms of using positive values and virtues to compensate for negative feelings, thoughts, or negative emotions. After researching further in this area, I was able to construct for the first time a Framework for the Rise of Humans comprised of Nine Stages. The Framework will be introduced later in this chapter. Refer to Figure 4.1.

Homi: Was there an intrinsic reason for your move in this direction or inclination to create the Framework?

Dr. Competence: The reason for this move was apparent. If I am going to help everyone follow their dreams and Life's Vision, they need to be free from life's issues that prevent them from pursuing their vision. To rise as a human, we need to free ourselves from this chain. Issues and problems in life are like a chain fastening our feet to the ground and thus restricting our movements. We can't rise as a human if we are chained to the ground. To free ourselves from the chains of issues, and grow as a member of one human family, we need a Framework to achieve such an end. In other words, it was necessary to have a Framework that achieves that sublime aim. A Framework enables every human being to deal with day-to-day issues and problems. It helps them discover the values that they may lack. We need to find these values for goal setting and supporting our vision. Therefore, my goal was to create a framework for this sublime purpose to bring humanity to love, light and unity through the fulfilment of their visions, which would lead to excellent results for everyone in our Human Family worldwide. Hence, as a researcher, I created a Framework for the Rise of Humans comprised of nine stages.

Homi: How did you come up with the nine stages?

Dr. Competence: The exciting part of the construction was that the final two stages were discovered and constructed first. The beginning stages of rising fulfilment were found and built later.

Homi: Why have you called it a Framework?

Dr. Competence: Because it is about work, whosoever is involved, needs to start to work on themselves using the Framework, so Framework is the best way to represent ROTH.

Homi: Okay, then, How does the Rise of The Humans Framework Work?

Rise of The Humans Framework (ROTH)

Dr. Competence: Using the Framework, we need to start from the first stage and work through all nine stages.

Homi: What happens at each stage?

Dr. Competence: At each stage, we rise higher and higher until we reach the heights of fulfilment by adopting the spirit of service we need to fulfil our vision.

Homi: How can we rise?

Dr. Competence: Each stage indicates the issues and problems that we must address to embrace our preferred visionary future. On the vision-driven path, we are entering a path of development and fulfilment while simultaneously pursuing goals. We seek the achievement of our goals to become, whilst at the same time going through the nine stages of the Framework.

Homi: Why do we need to work with issues while moving towards our Life's Vision?

Dr. Competence: Do not take it lightly, pursuing goals involves setbacks and brings our issues to the fore. The fulfilment of our vision is a process parallel to dealing with our issues to the last minute of rising fulfilment. The journey on the vision-driven path is similar to the railway lines or tracks. Both lines are parallel but crucial.

Homi: What each stage is comprised of?

Dr. Competence: Each stage of fulfilment consists of a Let Go Of or Dealing Limb, a Being Limb, and an Embracing Limb. We go through nine stages of rising fulfilment as human beings, refer to Figure 4.1. As human beings we are constantly dealing with issues, on a day-to-day basis, throughout our life. To deal with these issues properly, we need to embrace new values. These values help us in the pursuit of our vision. In other words, if the issues prevent us from moving forward, or hindering our progress, we must deal with them. The best way to deal with problems is to look at them through the lens of our values.

Homi: Do you mean the values are the lenses we see the world through?

Dr. Competence: Exactly, we see the world around us through the values we hold dear in our hearts, they are the lenses we have in pursuit of our vision.

Homi: What happens if we need to be stronger in some values?

Dr. Competence: If we are weak in a specific value, we need to energize it, if we do not have it, accept it as our value.

Homi: If we resist adopting specific values what happens?

Dr. Competence: If we resist accepting it, our issues persist and impede our progress on the Vision Driven Path, and our rise as a human. It is as simple as that.

Homi: Can you provide an example?

Dr. Competence: No problem. For example, consider that we are working on the first stage of the Framework, i.e. the "Be Brave" Stage. The first stage encourages us to be brave and have courage on the vision-driven path. So, to fulfil being courageous, we may have some fears to overcome to move ahead on the vision-driven path and rise. Maybe, we need to use our inner vision to look inside and identify the cause of not being brave.

Homi: How are we able to achieve that?

Dr. Competence: We need to reflect on the issue. While remembering we must scrutinize ourselves about which value is lacking and causing us such fear. We need to look within, meditate, sit in silence, reflect, and ask ourselves this question, "what is lacking?" knowing that by discovering and adopting the new value we end the fear and embrace courage. In the First Stage of the Framework, the "Be Brave" stage of fulfilment, we start to rise as humans and feel we are growing.

Homi: How joyful is this process of rising?

Dr. Competence: It gives us wings, it gives us wings, it gives us wings.

Homi: What happens after we have resolved the issues at the first stage of ROTH, and we have risen to a higher level of the Framework?

Dr. Competence: After we have risen to the next stage, i.e., the "Be Certain" stage, we commence our work similarly. We may pass this stage faster, or if we have issues at this level, we will need to pin down by finding out the opposing values.

Homi: Okay, and after we have discovered the new values, what do we do next?

Dr. Competence: Next, we need to adopt the new values. By embracing these values, we can practice them in our lives and, thus, become certain.

Homi: What is the main focus here at stage 2?

Dr. Competence: At this stage, we must deal with all the doubts preventing us from progressing.

Homi: What are the stages of the Rise Of The Humans (ROTH) Framework?

Dr. Competence: The nine stages of the Rise of Humans Framework are: Be Brave, Be Certain, Be Present, Be Social, Be Open, Be Accepting, Be Serving, Be Visionary, and Be Global.

Homi: What are the objectives of the ROTH Framework?

Dr. Competence: The whole spectrum of the framework is based on this premise: We need to work from stage 1 to 7 on the issues preventing us from fulfilling our Life's Vision. At stage seven we adopt the "Spirit of Service" and become empowered to fulfil our Life's Vision. In the following two stages of 8 and 9, we work on our Life's Vision with the acquired "Spirit of Service".

Homi: Do you mean that up to stage 7, we work on ourselves to acquire the Spirit of Service, then use the spirit of service to serve our clients, community and even the world?

Dr. Competence: Exactly: at Stage 7, we need to acquire the spirit of service to move on to the stage 8. At stage 8 we become visionary, meaning we can see the future clearly, vividly, bigger and better.

Homi: What is the final stage and what happens there?

Dr. Competence: After becoming a visionary at the stage 8, we are ready for the last stage "To let our vision be world Embracing".

Homi: What is our work at each stage of the Framework?

Dr. Competence: By focusing on our issues at each stage of the Rise of The Humans Framework, we realise that our problems are guiding us to find the missing values that are vital for our progress, success, and happiness. Many of our issues and concerns been caused by lacking these values.

Homi: What happens if we face new issues?

Dr. Competence: If any issue continues to become a hindrance, or if new problems arise and become barriers to our progress to fulfil our vision, we need to take action. We need to remember that by doing so we rise, again and again; each time we rise we discover and adopt a value that the absence of which has caused a problem. We need always remember that; our ultimate fulfilment is the fulfilment of our Life's Vision. We need to remember that our issues or problems slow down our progress towards the ultimate fulfilment, which is the fulfilment of our Life's Vision. We go through the Rise of The Humans Framework (ROTH) to rise as humans to fulfil and advance on the vision-driven path, as we ascend.

Homi: How can we discover our values without a coach, is this possible?

Dr. Competence: The coaches are great. However, if we can discover our values, according to the guidance of our inner vision based on resolving the issues or problems.

Homi: What if our parents or peers push us to accept and adopt specific values?

Dr. Competence: As we rise, we need to be on our guard that our values are genuinely ours and be vigilant not to adopt the values of others.

Homi: Therefore, as we find our missing values, we need to make sure that we practice them to rise. You may recall the story of my mother. As we rise, we will realise that many individuals still need to fulfil their vision, just like the story of my mother. Those people may feel regrets towards the end of their lives if they remain unable to change direction and fulfil their vision. When my mother was a child, she had her Life's Vision.

Dr. Competence: Children who had their dreams but were dissuaded by others and did not pursue their Life's Vision when they are grownups will remain unfulfilled. Let us gain knowledge and experience in discovering our vision. Let us rise as humans by going through the Stages of fulfilment, dealing with our issues, finding out the values we lack, and embracing our pride because we are in this life for a reason: to fulfil our Life's Vision and rise.

Rise of The Humans Framework (ROTH)

Homi: I agree, we need to avoid regrets by being courageous to take opportunities that come our way when we are on the vision-driven path.

Dr. Competence: Reflect for a moment on how many individuals have missed their opportunities because of all the values they lacked that were necessary for fulfilling Life's Vision.

Homi: Therefore, what is important to us is finding and listing our values as we rise on the Vision Driven Path using the Framework, right?

Dr. Competence: Of course, we need to list the values. We need to start with the issues we face now. To discover the values that fulfil our vision, and save our life. Our life and our Life's Vision are both important to us. These values can be found by us while working with the Rise of The Humans Framework (ROTH).

Homi: Okay, what heights are we able to reach? What can we expect?

Dr. Competence: ROTH explains how humans can rise to the heights of achievement by fulfilling their vision. There are 9 stages. At each stage, we climb higher until we reach the heights of fulfilment. As we are empowered to rise higher, we feel the power of fulfilment influences our minds, actions, and our entire being. As we ascend we realise we are closer to the heights of fulfilment. The rising stages are so inspiring we feel the joy of rising penetrating our entire being.

Homi: How do we feel when working at the different levels of ROTH? Are these stages inspiring?

Dr. Competence: The Stages of rising to different heights become so inspiring that we, as humans feel our whole existence become aflame, and we think our burning desire approaching fruition. And in our hearts and mind we feel the joy and the ecstasy of rising that penetrates every cell of our body.

Homi: Do we become confident as we rise?

Dr. Competence: Definitely, while we are rising, we become more confident in our lives as we feel our vision turns into a journey of becoming. It is a delightful journey. At every stage, the feeling of fulfilment penetrates our minds and soul. Every moment, everything we do becomes part of this enlightenment.

Homi: Those who want to pursue their vision wish to make their life meaningful. How meaningful is our work with ROTH?

Dr. Competence: As we rise, we realise that nothing is impossible for us anymore. We become so empowered that we can face any difficulty in life. As we face and overcome the challenges in our life, we realise further that we are indeed on a journey of transformation. In our transformation journey, joy and happiness feeds our minds, soul, and our body. This sensation or intuition becomes aflame, and as we approach the heights of fulfilment, our life becomes more meaningful, and we realise why we are in this life.

Homi: What are the benefits of this realisation?

Dr. Competence: The benefits of this realisation are as follows:

- We find ourselves on a journey of self-discovery and growth,
- All our uncertainties disappear,
- All our lost-ness will disappear
- At every stage, we find missing pieces
- We can see that all the pieces of the jigsaw puzzle of our life come together, and
- We gradually see the whole picture of why we are here, and
- This contributes to our transformation within the chrysalis of our Life's Vision.

Homi: Do you mean while we work with our issues at each level and discover and adopt and practice new values we transform?

Dr. Competence: As we transform through these nine stages within the chrysalis of our vision, soon, the time will be approaching, when we are ready to leave the old self. At each stage, we feel we are transforming into our new selves within the chrysalis until we reach the seventh stage, where we embrace the spirit of service. Equipped with the spirit of service, we are ready to move to the eighth level and become a visionary. Empowered by our Life's Vision, we ascend to stage nine, where we emerge like a butterfly to embrace the whole world.

Homi: You mean like a caterpillar transforming in the chrysalis and emerging as a butterfly throughout the ROTH Framework.

Dr. Competence: Precisely, like a butterfly, when at stage seven, we acquire the spirit of service, we are now ready to serve people around us, our clients, customers and so forth. And after that we are ready for the grand finale, the most meaningful stage in our life, of embracing the world through our vision. By becoming, we have fulfilled our dream. Now we can serve.

Homi: What is the similarity of serving to the emerging butterfly?

Dr. Competence: When a caterpillar becomes a butterfly, it can serve the flowers. Similar to us, a caterpillar's vision is fulfilled when it transforms into a butterfly. A butterfly's purpose is to serve the flowers of the world as this is so meaningful for its life.

Homi: Is this meaningfulness and fulfilment of our Life's Vision interrelated?

Dr. Competence: Yes, let me explain: As we come to grasp the meaningfulness of our vision, we see that our life has been transformed and becomes so meaningful, like the butterfly's life, that we have never imagined it this way before. As we let our vision be world-embracing, we reach the culmination of this meaningfulness. As the dimensions of this meaningfulness expand, we will find ourselves flying to the heights of fulfilment.

Homi: What is next that we can discuss?

Dr. Competence: I suggest we go through the next few pages that explain ROTH. We will arrange another meeting about how to work with ROTH.

Homi: That is great, see you for that discussion in a few days.

The Rise of the Humans Framework is comprised of nine stages, as illustrated in the following figure:

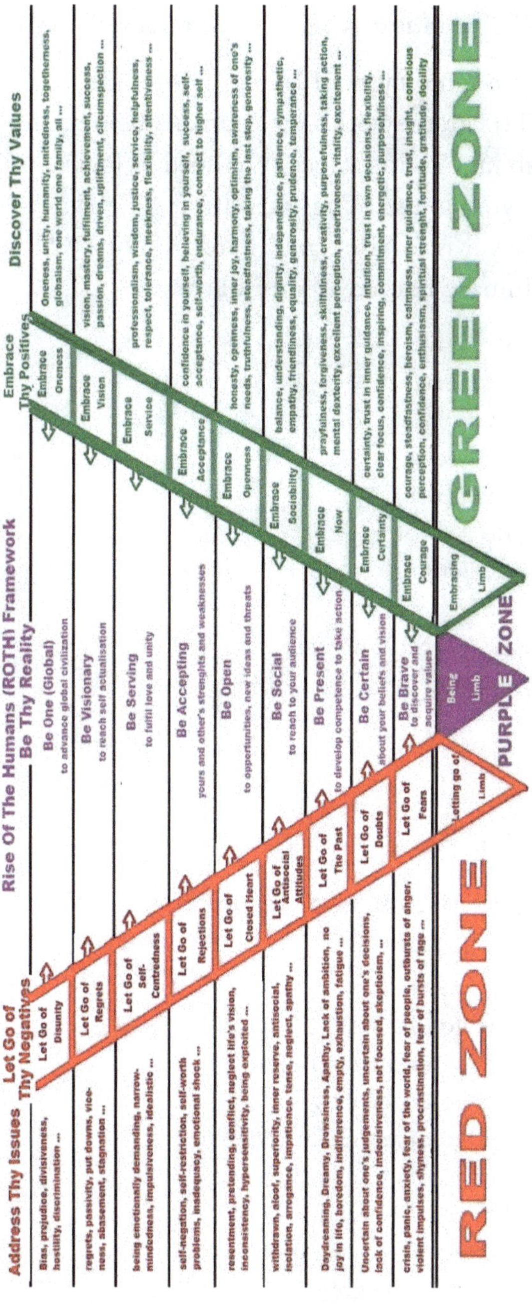

Rise of The Humans Framework (ROTH)

Figure 4.1 – The Rise of The Humans (ROTH) Framework

Rise Of The Humans (ROTH) Framework

There are nine stages of Being, in the Rise Of The Humans (ROTH) Framework. As human beings, we are going through nine Being stages. We need to focus on Being, more than anything else. The question is "To Be or Not to Be"? The answer is to "Be', and there are Nine "BE's" in Rise of The Humans Framework as follows:

1. Be Brave
2. Be Certain
3. Be Present
4. Be Social
5. Be Open
6. Be Accepting
7. Be Serving
8. Be Visionary
9. Be World Embracing

The Framework has three Limbs

1. Letting go of
2. Being
3. Embracing

Letting go of Limb also, is comprised of Nine "Let Go Of" parts, as follows:

1. Let go of fears
2. Let go of uncertainties
3. Let go of the past
4. Let go of antisocial behaviors
5. Let go of closed heart
6. Let go of Rejections
7. Let go of self-centeredness
8. Let go of Regrets
9. Let go of Disunity

Embracing Limb, similarly, is comprised of nine embraces as follows:

1. Embrace Courage
2. Embrace Certainty
3. Embrace Present
4. Embrace Sociability
5. Embrace Openness
6. Embrace Acceptance
7. Embrace Service
8. Embrace Vision
9. Embrace Oneness

The arrows are pointing to the centre of the ROTH Framework. Letting go of our issues and embracing our values allows us to move to the centre being humans in all nine levels or stages of Being.

The nine stages of the Framework, are summarized in the following paragraphs:

I - Be Brave,

"Courage is rightly considered the foremost of the virtues for upon it all others depend"
Winston Churchill

If you remember the first regret that people listed before dying was, "I wish I'd had the courage to live a life true to myself". So, we need to be brave on the vision driven path, we must deal with issues preventing us from being courageous. Fear is a negative emotion. Negative emotion indicates a lack, like the darkness is the absence of light. It is holding us back and preventing us from rising as a human beings. All sorts of fears may come our way in our life. Before Rise of the Humans Framework (ROTH), we may have looked at fear as, "Forget Everything and Run' (F.E.A.R.).

For example, the fear of darkness. Why do we have a fear of darkness? Because the lack of light has created a question; is there someone or something in the dark? You do not know; no one knows. Not knowing creates fear. Therefore, it is proved that a lack of light or knowledge has led to fear. In this case, we have three lacks:

- A Lack of light,
- A Lack of knowledge of the dark area,
- A Lack of knowledge about wild animals or things that might be there.

In such circumstances, we tend to, "Forget Everything and Run".

Hence, fear has resulted from a lack, and we tend to Forget Everything and Run. Fear is a lack of value and nothing else. Therefore, values are light, issues and problems are darkness, and the solution is discovering the light to enlighten the soul. When we act to create the light, the darkness goes. When we act by changing the darkness into light, we have given fear a new meaning: "**Face Everything and Rise**' (F.E.A.R.). When we do that, we feel that fear now has a new meaning. We cannot even see the issue anymore because the darkness has disappeared, as there is only light, and we are rising.

When we have risen our view is from the heights and different from the previous view we had before rising. I remember memories of my youth as a mountain climber; when we reached the higher levels, we had a larger and different view of the landscape than we did before rising to those heights. We continue to see it by the light until this becomes our habit. Aristotle stated, "Moral excellence comes about as a result of habit". We become just by believing and adopting the new meaning of fear, i.e., Face Everything And Rise', that is applicable in the Rise of the Humans Framework, the ROTH framework, reflecting and focusing on this new meaning of fear which is Facing Everything and Rise. It is new thinking by doing, such as becoming brave by performing brave acts.

For example, we need to discover what values are essential to deal with our fear and nullify or neutralise the effect. When we find out and list these values are the most important ones in our lives to remove the brake that is holding us back and our progression to fulfilment.

By fulfilling stage one, we rise again to the next level. This, describes the process of rising as humans. We need to detach from anything that holds us down and prevents us from rising as humans. Suppose a negative issue that is holding us down, or we realise that it is a hindrance. In that case, we need to deal with it by discovering a value we resist adopting, to achieve and maintain our balance in life.

Remember at each stage of the Rise of The Humans Framework (ROTH), we rise higher and higher. At stage seven, our aim is to embrace the spirit of service. After embracing the spirit of service, the two stages are "Be Visionary" and "Be Global". Visionary means seeing the future more significant, more transparent, and more promising than before. Adopting the Spirit of Service is a passage or a bridge leading us to the Spirit of Oneness in the ninth stage.

The Ninth Stage, of the ROTH Framework, being the last, is to let our vision be world embracing. Why? Because here is the fact that whether you are a business owner, a worker, a politician, a professional, or functioning at any capacity in the present time, your clients, customers, fans, friends, etc., come from all over the world. You see that you need to embrace the world and adopt the spirit of oneness with them to function, live and prosper. Adopting the spirit of oneness is ultimate stage of our development as human beings.

Because there is lack, human beings need to be charged with the light of courage or a value that can enlighten the situation about a number of things in their lives. Therefore, if we fear something like the fears listed in the ROTH, we need to illuminate the fear with the dazzling light of (values) to re-balance and rise to the next level.

If we are fearful, we are not ready to rise higher and continue our journey on the vision-driven path. The fear holds us down and prevents us from moving forward. It may cause us to freeze. We need to grow as human beings on the vision-driven path and acquire values that befit our Life's Vision. The remedy is to "Be Brave', be courageous, and exercise bravery by adopting and owning our values Values are our lights, uplifting, enlightening, and making us rise as ourselves. To be brave human beings on the vision-driven Path, we must be ourselves. And not copy or imitate someone else. We need to become our authentic selves These are what we need as our lights. Refer to Figure 4.1.

When we become the seeker of light, we discover weighty enlightening values at every moment of our journey on the vision-driven path working within the Rise of The Humans Framework. We become aware of the mystery of rediscovering ourselves. Because at every step on the vision-driven path, we might discover a new light that enlightens the darkness of fears. It helps us see there was an imagined fear and nothing else.

Be Brave stage, is the first level of heaven of fulfilment. By fulfilling the first level, we rise up to the next. In other words, in the process of rising as humans we need to detach from any issues between us and our Life's Vision. We need to deal with any problem holding us down. If an issue is a hindrance, we need to deal with it by adopting a value that sheds light on our life.

As we rise higher like an eagle, we need to spread our wings in the full force of our values. If we roll up our wings to rest at that height, we descend towards the ground. We need to keep our wings spread open. As each value we hold is likened to is a feather in our wings, the beauty of reaching heights, just like an eagle, requires more feathers. Because personality and ego coexist, throwing all the negatives in our way that must be dealt with, we must always be prepared to adopt values and spread our wings as we soar. We are dealing with some issues and problems at this level.

By adopting one or more of the values, by throwing light into the darkness of issues, we start to rise. We are climbing higher into this realm of being and advancing on the vision-driven path towards our fulfilment. We feel lighter and think we are becoming lovers of light. We are becoming ourselves each step of the way, and at each rising. And if with the help of our inner vision, we discover all the lights needed for our growing, we shall soar into the heaven of Certainty.

Some of the issues affecting us at this level are as follows:
- Crisis
- Panic
- Anxiety
- Fear of the world
- Fear of people
- Outbursts of anger
- Violent impulses
- Shyness
- Procrastination
- Fear of bursts of rage
- Unknown fears
- Superstitions

Before we are ready to rise higher to the certainty level, we need to enlighten our fears with the lights of one or more of the values as listed in the Rise of The Humans Framework (ROTH) which are as follows:

1. Courage
2. Steadfastness
3. Heroism
4. Calmness
5. Inner guidance
6. Trust
7. Insight
8. Conscious perception
9. Confidence
10. Enthusiasm
11. Spiritual Strength
12. Fortitude
13. Gratitude
14. Docility
15. Balance

16. Personal Development
17. Spirituality

II – Be Certain,

The next level is **"Be Certain"**. The uncertainties we have already learned about and rated ourselves in from the first chapter need to be dealt with as we rise.

Again, to become certain and embrace certainty we need to deal with our issues and develop a number of new Values, or we may need to adopt from this category a number of values that help us become certain. Without certainty we are halted in our life and unable to proceed and follow our vision and calling. We need to figure out our issues and resolve them. In that case, we can refer to Rise of The Humans Framework (ROTH), Figure 4.1, to see whether we might be struggling with any of the listed issues.

We need to clear our fears to become ready to work with our uncertainties. If we are sure, particularly about our direction, we can always be confident about what we are doing in our lives. If we are both fearful and uncertain, matters get worse. Therefore, we must clear our fears and work on fears before we continue working on other issues. For example, we have a problem with trust at the level of working with fears. In that case, we need to be free of those fears by developing the quality, virtue or value called, "Trustfulness" first.

Again, to become certain and embrace certainty we need to deal with a number of negativities and develop a number of new Values, or at least one value. We need to adopt a value that helps us become certain. Without certainty we are halted in our life and unable to proceed and follow our vision and calling. If we are unsure about some issues, we can refer to Rise of The Humans Framework (ROTH) Figure 4.1, as stated above.

For example, the value called trust has been listed at first and second levels. Suppose we are dealing with issues that make us doubtful. In that case we need to identify those issue in the Framework. One of the issues is being, "Uncertain in own judgement". If this is the problem we are struggling with at this level, we need to determine which value will light up this issue. Let's assume we discover that we don't trust our inner guidance or vision. This discovery relieves us from the problem, and we can move into balance.

In everyday life we are constantly making a number of small or big decisions. If we are uncertain about our vision, we are not able to make the right decisions or act on our choices.

What is the solution? The simple answer is that we need to deal with all sorts of issues leading to uncertainties and embrace certainty. As a result, we will achieve a number of values and qualities that will help us to live a life of happiness free of uncertainties.

At this level, you are dealing with some issues too. Some of the issues that you might have problems with are as follows:

- Uncertain about one's judgements
- Uncertain about one's decisions
- Lack of confidence
- Indecisiveness
- Not focused
- Skepticism

- Pessimism
- Lack of confidence
- Giving up
- Resignation
- Stagnation
- Exhaustion
- Lack of enthusiasm
- Lack of goals
- Vague Goals
- Lack of direction
- Lack of vision

Before we are ready to rise and to work on our issues at the "Being Present" stage of the Rise Of The Humans (ROTH) Framework, we need to clear our uncertainties. Some of the relevant values and qualities that we can discover, develop, adopt, and practice at this level are:

18. Certainty
19. Trust in inner guidance
20. Intuition
21. Trust in own decisions
22. Flexibility
23. Clear Focus
24. Confidence
25. Inspiring
26. Commitment
27. Energetic
28. Purposefulness
29. Good Judgement
30. Obedience to Higher Self
31. Vision

32. Beliefs
33. Direction
34. Self-trust
35. Inspiration
36. Energetic
37. Clarity

III – Be Present

We need to be present on the vision-driven path, so we must to deal with issues that prevent us from being present. We can take action, develop skills, or become competent, in the present, not in the past or in the future. We have to be in the present, to continue working on our personal development. We need to be in the present to develop competencies, learn new skill and act. Why? Because the past is gone and whatever action we take happens in the present time. We can plan for the future in the present. After we have cleared our fears and uncertainties, we need to clear the issues around our living in the present. Why? Because the good news is we are now courageous and certain and now we are ready to address the problems which have been preventing us from BEING PRESENT. Some of these issues are as follows:

- Daydreaming
- Dreamy
- Drowsiness
- Apathy
- Lack of ambition
- No Joy in life
- Boredom
- Indifference

- Empty
- Exhaustion
- Fatigue
- Incessant inner dialogue
- Incompetent

In other words, we are brave, we achieved "Courageousness' and certainty. Now we are ready to deal with the issues preventing us from living in the present and being happy. We may not be satisfied because of something or some ways of thinking in our present circumstances. Maybe we are living in the past and not in the present, we are thinking about the good old times or something that makes us go back in our mind to the past, and when we do this, we are no longer in the present.

Although the power of now is here for us to use, we cannot. Or we may have no interest in the current moment. Maybe we are indifferent about things that are happening now. If this is our problem, we need to resolve it otherwise we experience a happy feeling. Although we may know how we feel about the present and how it is possible to do something about it, we may do nothing and just let time passes by.

Why are we not doing something in the present that would make us feel better? There might be something that we know deep down or a negative feeling about something that makes us sad or prevents us from being jolly and having enthusiasm. We need to find it and uproot it by acquiring powerful values that enlighten us to do what we love and make us have inner unity. Remember values are the lights that enlighten our darkness.

Because we live in the now / the present, if any issues are interfering with our living in the present, all these issues must be dealt with by acquiring new values and embracing our competence. In other words, we need to deal with issues preventing us from having a joyful time living our life with the best possibilities. That is our right.

Before we are ready to move higher to the 'Be Social' level, we need to deal with the issues by adopting further Values, some of which are listed below:

38. Prayerfulness
39. Forgiveness
40. Skilfulness
41. Creativity
42. Purposefulness
43. Taking action
44. Mental Dexterity
45. Excellent Perception
46. Assertiveness
47. Vitality
48. Excitement
49. Enthusiasm
50. Perseverance
51. Command
52. Magnanimity
53. Embrace opportunity
54. Good Health
55. Longevity
56. Inner Guidance
57. Competence
58. Confidence
59. Freedom

IV – Be Social

We need to be social on the vision-driven path, so we need to deal with issues that prevent us from embracing sociability. You may be aware of these socially related issues. Some of these issues are listed for your awareness:

- Withdrawn
- Aloof
- Superiority
- Inner Reserve
- Antisocial
- Isolation
- Arrogance
- Impatience
- Tense
- Neglect
- Apathy
- Indifference
- Loneliness
- Negative Criticism

After we have sorted out the issues regarding being present, we are now rising to a higher level, and we are now able to deal with the problems at the level of "being social". At this level we can start with family issues as well as issues with our friends, and community. In general, we like to feel at ease and comfortable with the community we are in and be able to integrate socially. These issues may be a few, but if they persist, it is our responsibility to clear and deal with them, recover from them, and rise higher as human beings.

THE RISE OF THE HUMANS

We may feel, at this level, that we like to be left alone. However, this is an issue. Remember to grow as a human, we need to address our problems at all levels and rise.

By working through these issues aiming at being social and embracing sociability, we need to realise that we may lack one or more values at this level that we need to explore, discover, adopt and practice in our lives.

By working through these issues aiming at being social and embracing sociability, we need to realise that we may lack one or more values at this level that we need to explore, discover, adopt and practice in our lives. We can rise higher as human beings by finding the values we need and adopting them in our lives. When we grow this way, we feel united with them. It is an uplifting feeling that we have never experienced before.

Before we move to higher levels, we need to deal with issues at the sociability level, neutralising our negative feelings practising our values at this level and bringing ourselves to balance.

60. Balance
61. Understanding
62. Dignity
63. Independence
64. Patience
65. Sympathetic
66. Empathy
67. Friendliness
68. Equality
69. Generosity
70. Prudence

71. Temperance
72. Modesty
73. Purity
74. Clemency
75. Kindness
76. Love
77. Patience
78. Moderation
79. Courtesy
80. Affability
81. Tolerance
82. Compassion
83. Equality
84. Sociable

V - Be Open

As we need to be open on the vision-driven path, we must deal with issues that prevent us from embracing opportunities. When we feel comfortable socially and at ease no matter the circumstances, we will communicate and participate better in more groups and situations (compared to if we felt uncomfortable socially). Now that we function well socially by having acquired the qualities listed above, we feel we are rising again to a new height, to the Stage of **"Being Open"**.

At this level of growth, we can open our minds to opportunities, move mountains and make things happen. We can achieve our goals. We may strongly feel that we are moving in the direction of our Life's Vision, and rising to the heights of fulfilment with an open mind.

If there are issues that impede us from maintaining an open mind, we clear these issues by working with the Rise of The Humans Framework (ROTH).

We are well aware that we are able now to communicate freely and socially. We acknowledge that we deserve congratulations because reaching these heights is a considerable achievement. Why? Because so far, we have acquired and adopted many Core Values that are our guiding principles and the source of inspiration. We now feel great, knowing that whenever we encounter issues, we are able to comfortably deal with them.

At this level, we are also aware that we need to address those issues by acquiring even more values, as our ammunition, on the vision-driven path and as we rise higher and higher. We have learned to find those issues stopping us from embracing the opportunities around us and the opportunities coming our way. Some of these issues are listed as follows:

- Resentment
- Pretending
- Conflict
- Neglect Life's Vision
- Inconsistency
- Hypersensitivity
- Being exploited
- Being Persuaded
- Dissuaded
- Vacillation
- Rage
- Jealousy

- Envy
- Revenge
- Suspicious
- Vexation
- Anger
- Led Astray
- Hatred

Before we are ready to move to the Acceptance stage, where we practice accepting and embracing our strengths, we need to deal with the issues at the Open mindedness level to rise higher. We become open to "Embracing Opportunity" by acquiring new values, some of which are listed below, that throw light into the darkness of negativity, nullifying the effects of our negative feelings at this level as follows:

85. Honesty
86. Openness
87. Inner Joy
88. Harmony
89. Optimism
90. Awareness of one's needs
91. Truthfulness
92. Steadfastness
93. Taking the last step
94. Generosity
95. Goodwill
96. Love
97. Inner Harmony
98. Understanding
99. Peacefulness
100. Sincerity

101. Foresight
102. Warm Heartedness

VI - Be Accepting

Accepting beings embrace their strengths

To be able to accept, we must find issues preventing us from being so. We must accept ourselves and acknowledge our strengths and weaknesses. We need to accept others and the circumstances around us. Rejection is the opposite of acceptance. To be accepting requires the adoption and practice of specific values.

As we must practice accepting and letting go of rejection on the vision driven path, we must deal with issues preventing us from embracing our strengths. It is by resolving these issues through discovering and adopting the values at this level that we rise again as humans. Remember in the Rise of The Humans Framework, we rise by exercising our values to address our issues. Our issues at this level guide us to discover the values that pertain at this height, which are as follows:

- Self-negation
- Self-restriction
- Self-worth problems
- Inadequacy
- Emotional shock
- Bitterness
- Exhaustion
- Despondency
- Anxiety

As we pursue our Life's Vision, we may learn more about our strengths and weaknesses. If we accept our weaknesses, we can and are able to deal with them or find a way to overcome them. We also need to rely on our strengths to cope with any unforeseen situations that may arise. Accepting both our strengths and weaknesses will definitely assist us in overcoming any obstacles on the vision-driven path towards the fulfilment of our Life's Vision.

With this understanding, we have reached an advanced stage. Congratulations! At this stage we need to work on accepting ourselves, accepting others and the world around us and in this way, we need to embrace our strengths. Acceptance of others also includes acceptance of their strengths and weaknesses. Everyone has some strengths and some flaws, and no one is perfect.

Before we enter the next phase, we need to accept ourselves and all the work we have done so far for our vision on the vision-driven path and concerning people around us. Our team, colleagues, family, friends, and community even extend it to the world of humanity where we live. We need to truly accept that we have come a long way on the vision-driven path and we are close to fulfilling our vision.

Before we are ready to move to embrace the spirit of service, must deal with any issues of acceptance. This means using our power to accept ourselves and the people around us through the eyes of acceptance.

We need to ensure that no trace of negativity is left and all the issues that bar us from accepting them are wiped out from our hearts. The process of Being Accepting requires us to deal with the problems by embracing our strengths, leading to the acquisition of values, some of which are as follows:

103. Confidence in yourself
104. Believing in yourself
105. Success
106. Self-acceptance
107. Self-worth
108. Endurance
109. Connect to higher self
110. Constructiveness
111. Commitment
112. Creativity
113. Joyfulness
114. Coping
115. Connection
116. Commitment
117. Skilfulness
118. Spirituality
119. Strength
120. Prosperity
121. Responsibility
122. Loyalty

VII - Be Serving

Remember, at each stage of the Rise of The Humans Framework (ROTH), we rise higher and higher. At stage seven our aim is to embrace the spirit of service. After acquiring the spirit of service, the two stages are "Be Visionary' and "Be World Embracing'. Visionary means seeing the future as more significant, transparent, and more promising than before. The ninth stage, the last one, is to let our vision be world-embracing.

As we need to be of service on the vision-driven path, we must deal with issues that prevent us from embracing the spirit of service. We have now arrived at the level of service. At this level, we are ready to serve our family, friends, customers, clients, community, and society. If we have a business, this is where businesspeople, and those involved in business, can function better when they also clear the issues they may have at this level. Again, some of these issues are as follows, as listed in Figure 4.1.

The following are some of the issues:

- Being emotionally demanding
- Narrow-mindedness
- Possessiveness
- Impulsiveness
- Idealistic
- Pitiless
- Prejudiced
- Judgmental
- Irritated
- Critical of others
- See imperfections

Remember always that you need to flood yourself with the values, then acquire and adopt them as your own core values, flooding the faults (which are against the spirit of service) you have discovered in yourself to embrace the spirit of service.

So, in dealing with these issues and washing them away from our being, we need to acquire the appropriate values and adopt them as our own.

This level is the station of service, service to our audience and customers. Service to those around us and to humanity. This stage of service is given to those you have in mind from the inception of your vision.

At this level, too, we acquire new values and develop virtues. We are enriching the repertoire of values which we are operating from. Some of these values are listed underneath:

123. Professionalism
124. Wisdom
125. Justice
126. Service
127. Helpfulness
128. Respect
129. Tolerance
130. Meekness
131. Flexibility
132. Attentiveness
133. Spontaneity
134. Lenience
135. Empathy
136. Mental Acuity
137. Understanding
138. Enthusiasm
139. Inspiring
140. Loving
141. Patience
142. Interest for Business
143. Interest to have a career
144. Justice
145. Rule of Law,
146. Integrity

VIII - Be Visionary

After we have risen to this height, we have acquired the spirit of service. However, we are also aware that at this highest level, we still have issues to deal with. By adopting the spirit of service, we are ready to embrace the power of our Life's Vision. The problems we are dealing with at this level could be much less because we have already dealt with many. Some of the issues could be as follows:

- Regrets
- Passivity
- Put downs
- Vice-ness
- Abasement
- Stagnation
- Decline
- Despise

To soar at this height is so uplifting that you feel you are on top of the world. You feel like gazing down, to enjoy the view, the landscape, the beauty. It is unbelievable! the joy you think may be challenging to put into words is sublime. With few exceptions, you can't compare this joy to any other pleasures in life.

As we have realised on our journey, issues are like our mentors, or our guides, leading us to light of values to balance our life. This approach to self-development helps us grow and advance on the vision-driven path. Some of these values are as follows:

147. Vision
148. Mastery
149. Fulfilment
150. Achievement
151. Success
152. Passion
153. Dreams
154. Driven
155. Upliftment
156. Circumspection
157. Industriousness
158. Diligence
159. Orderliness
160. Becoming
161. Purposeful
162. Realisation
163. Greatness
164. Highest Aspiration
165. Blessed
166. Glorious
167. Enlightened
168. Exemplar

IX – Be One

Bahaullah emphasized that we need to," let our Vision be world Embracing". Rising to this level requires that we be aware of the pitfall of the issues that may surround us and hold us down or impede our progress. Even at this level we need to deal with issues and enlighten ourselves with values that uplift us and make us rise.

Rise of The Humans Framework (ROTH)

Remember that the aim of working through the framework is twofold:

Firstly, on our journey to discover our vision to fulfil, we need to find our core values. Our core or primary values need to be placed next to what we love, and what our talents are, to help us discover our vision.

Secondly, we rise higher and higher at each stage of the Rise of The Humans Framework (ROTH). At stage seven, our aim is to embrace the spirit of service. After adopting the spirit of service, the next two stages are "Be Visionary' and "Be World Embracing'. Visionary means seeing the future as more significant, transparent, and promising than before.

The Ninth Stage of the ROTH Framework, being the last, is to let our vision be world-embracing. Why? Because here is the fact, whether you have a business, or a job, or you are a politician, or you are a professional, no matter what capacity you function in right now, your clients or customers, or fans or friends come from all over the world, and if you want your business or work to continue to function, live and prosper well in this type of world then you need to embrace the world and adopt the spirit of oneness. To adopt the spirit of oneness is the ultimate stage of our development as human beings.

Some of the issues that can pull us down that we need to deal with or avoid are as follows:
- Bias
- Prejudice
- Divisiveness
- Hostility
- Discrimination

- Separation
- War
- Dominion
- Antagonism

This is the final level of the Rise Of The Humans (ROTH) Framework. It is the culmination of all levels of rising fulfilment, the stages that helped us to soar higher and higher are now well below our wings. We have become eagles with the massive power of vision. We have flown to these heights. It is unimaginable. As we feel that, we are soaring in the heavens of grandeur. At every moment of being at these heights, we wonder about our growth. Now we may feel dumbfounded by the beauty of creation as we look around and beneath our wings. It seems like a dream come true. We are in a different world. It is a world that we have embraced with our vision. At these heights we can adopt one or some of the following values:

169. Oneness
170. Unity
171. Humanity
172. Unitedness
173. Togetherness
174. Globalism
175. One world one family
176. All
177. One world family
178. One human race
179. Unity in diversity
180. Global community
181. Global market

182. Internationalism
183. Earth as one home
184. Extraordinaire
185. Spirit of oneness

ROTH Framework, in a nutshell, tells us that life is all about who we will become through the pains of life's issues that have broken our hearts or might have been burning us down in the RED ZONE. The best way out or remedy is to balance this by adopting values or virtues from the GREEN ZONE that works like water or a cooling mechanism. By this balancing effort, we will be able to act in the purple zone as human beings to be braver, more certain, more present, more social, more open, more accepting, more serving, more visionary and more united to finally become one with ourselves and the world.

THE RISE OF THE HUMANS

Chapter 5
How to work with ROTH

If we have the knowledge, skills, and money to invest, but we do not have the right attitudes, values and attributes, we are not able to rise. This is because our values form our virtual wings, and with our virtual wings, we can soar to the heights we desire. Why? Because our values draw people to us, our values are the cause of the fulfilment of our Life's Vision. People would like to do business and have some kind of relationship with us based on our values.

It has been about five days since I last met Dr. Competence. I was invited to a function on a Friday Night. It was a function where students and teachers meet casually to have dinner and play chess and other games. I also heard that they all bring their own dishes and share.

I arrived earlier and was chatting with some PhD students who were studying to complete their courses. After about 20 minutes many guests arrived and the hall was almost full, but I still couldn't see Dr. Competence. Small groups were engaged in stimulating discussions at every corner of the room. The buzz was very audible and uplifting.

I was scanning the crowd looking for Dr. Competence's face. Soon, I spotted him arriving at the door in the distance. I followed him with my eyes and started moving through the crowd towards him. Drinks and food were being offered all around. As I approached, I could see some people were engaging Dr. Competence in a conversation. By the time I reached the spot, he was now conversing with just a few people. He noticed me and I waved to him. Later, when an opportunity presented itself, I approached him. My aim was to make arrangements to continue our work on the Framework.

Homi: Hi, it is nice to see you here at this gathering, how are you? I want to talk to you, before you leave.

Dr. Competence: Great, I am fine, it is a little bit noisy here, can we go out on the terrace for a couple of minutes?

Homi: Sure

We walked out onto the terrace and continued our conversation.

Dr. Competence: I was thinking of talking to you about the Framework.

Homi: Me too, what about it?

Dr. Competence: Well, I think the Framework is great, it will help those who are on the vision driven path to discover their values and build on it.

"The following three paragraphs explain how the ROTH works, please read and see whether you also agree" Dr. Competence said as he handed me a dog-eared paper with hand-written notes.

I grabbed the paper and took a look.

How to work with ROTH

How does the Rise of The Humans Framework work?

Rising as a human requires developing, nurturing and owning values, not lacking values. Values are our inner assets. Values that are lacking in us appears as life issues that we are constantly struggling with. The struggle means we are out of balance. Discovering our values and adopting and practicing them in our lives is crucial. Our issues prevent us from being who we are and want to become.

When we are held down by issues, we cannot rise, fly high and reach the heights of fulfilment. We can't get to our destination, we cannot fulfil our vision, and we end up with regrets. Our issues persist in guiding us to discover our values. We can bring ourselves into balance, by adopting and welcoming those values in to our lives.

If we are chained down and incapable of reaching our full potential, we have a disability. As a result, we are not able to rise as a human. Hence, we should free ourselves from this cage, this bondage, and chain and seize our chance to grow. This is a prerequisite to the Rise of the Humans; it is a prerequisite to advance towards fulfilling our Life's Vision that leads us to rise as humans.

The ROTH Framework helps individuals discover their values and deal with the crippling issues that sometimes push us to the edge of the cliff of hopelessness. We need to save ourselves and our lives by discovering and adopting values.

The foundation of the ROTH is based on polarity of practicing values and the tendency to hang on to issues in our life. From when we are born to when we die, we deal with problems, and develop new qualities and values. This process continues throughout our whole life. In other words, while we are constantly dealing with issues of everyday life, we are also at the same time embracing new qualities and values as human being, to be able to "BE". It is the question of "TO BE OR NOT TO BE" when we follow our vision. It is this polarity that we face as human beings. We wrestle with this daily, throughout our whole life and whilst pursuing of our Life's Vision.

Shakespeare provided an example of this. Prince Hamlet had been facing his issues and troubles in the first six words of the Shakespearian's soliloquy, "TO BE OR NOT TO BE". Hamlet had actually been pondering whether or not to end his life. Perhaps this shows he did not have access to the ROTH framework. In any case, Hamlet lacked some essential values he needed to adopt and practise to achieve balance in his life. Given the many challenges that Hamlet was dealing with, the only action one can take against such problems is to revitalise and re-invigorate one's life by letting go of the negatives we hang on to and instead discovering and practising new qualities and positive values. That's the only way to balance the crippling issues we may face in life. When we do this, we become empowered.

Our issues become hinder our progress unless we face our issues on the Vision Driven Path and deal with them appropriately. Suppressing the issues or problems does not get us anywhere. These persisting issues indicate that we lack a value or virtue that we must adopt but have chosen to resist adopting.

Homi: Great, I had a quick read, I agree with what is on this piece of paper. Thank you for writing about it.

Dr. Competence: Did you notice the word persisting issue rather than issue that I referred to in the note?

Homi: Yes, I agree that when an issue persists, problems start to show up, we continuously feel trapped in the issue, and I agree it becomes like a chain that holds us down and cripples us. The persisting issues become so crippling that they slow and even stop the progress of our vision.

Dr. Competence: Definitely

Homi: How many approaches are there when using ROTH

Dr. Competence: There are three approaches when we work with the ROTH framework: Approach 1, Approach 2, and the Hybrid Approach.

Homi: What is Approach 1, and when can we use this Approach?

Dr. Competence: Approach 1 is used whenever we want to work on our life's issues as a guide to discover our values.

Homi: What about Approach 2, what is approach 2, and when can we use this Approach?

Dr. Competence: Approach 2 is used when we do not want to work with our life's issues, but are interested in discovering our values. In other words, in Approach 2 we work with ROTH to discover our values without touching on our life's issues.

Homi: What are the benefits of Approach 1?

Dr. Competence: The benefits are that while you are dealing with the issues that are affecting your life, you will learn how to balance your life. Balancing your life leads to discovering new values that you use to fulfil your Life's Vision. Therefore, in Approach 1 – You work on your life's issues and values.

Homi: What about Approach 2, what does this approach involve?

Dr. Competence: In Approach 2, work is only required on the Values. This is for people who feel that their issues are not interfering with or stopping their progress towards fulfilling of their vision. This group can use ROTH to discover their values without touching on their problems. They are needed to focus on finding their values.

Homi: What about the Hybrid Approach?

Dr. Competence: The Hybrid Approach is when we use both Approaches. We can use a Hybrid of both Approaches because the objective is to develop a list of values. Therefore, we can use Approach 1 for Some levels and Approach 2 for others. Because we may not have issues at all levels, but we still need values at those levels where we do not have problems.

Homi: Okay, so which Approach do we start with?

Dr. Competence: I think, we better start by focusing on Approach 1.

Homi: We need to explain each approach in a couple of Paragraphs before we provide an example of how practically we can use the approaches. If you agree with me, let's start.

Dr. Competence: I agree, it makes sense. Okay, here we are. I have already prepared this explanation regarding Approach 1:

ROTH–Approach 1, addressing the issues

The Rise of The Humans Framework is created to help us to have a balanced life. In Approach 1, we start by focusing on life's issues. There are always a number of issues that are affecting our life. These issues could be severe or not so intense. Still, they affect us at the nine levels illustrated in the Rise of The Humans Framework. Although these issues are cumbersome, we can use them as a guide to find the values, neutralise the problems, and bring our lives into balance before we pursue our vision. The values discovered in this process are needed for our further development empowering us to rise as humans to the heights of fulfilment in our lives.

The reason we need to work with the ROTH is very apparent: we need to deal with issues that are affecting us day and night and have created imbalances in our lives. The problems preventing us from progressing make us procrastinate or even give up what we are here to pursue, achieve and realise. By addressing these issues, we can be free and empowered by the new values to balance these issues. These values are critical for our progress.

Therefore, the result of sorting out and addressing the issues will be a list of values that are lacking in our lives. This lack shows why we have had the problems in the first place. These issues prevent us from progressing and fulfilling our destiny. We must clear the problems that cause us to give up and be unfulfilled. You will learn how to use the Rise of The Humans Framework to achieve such an outcome. Before progressing, learning about how to work with the ROTH to resolve your life's issues is essential. This work paves the way to the critical values you need to succeed.

Homi: That was a great explanation of Approach 1. Now, the question is, where do we start in the ROTH-Approach 1?

Dr. Competence: The very first thing to do when working with the ROTH-Approach 1 is to deal with our life issues and challenges at each level of the ROTH framework. There could be many issues or challenges that we are struggling with or confronting in our lives. These are contributing to an imbalance in our life:

Homi: Okay, what are the steps in ROTH-Approach 1

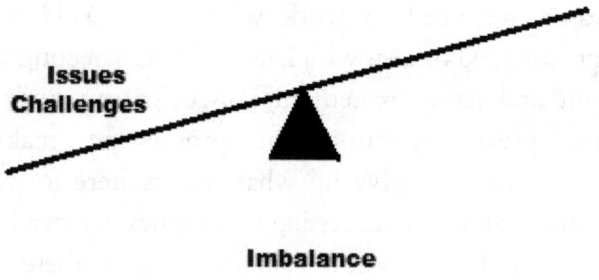

Figure 5.1 – The Imbalance

Dr. Competence: There are seven steps, as follows:

I -Write a short story about your situation
II-Underline the issues/problems
III-Which level does the issue belong to?
IV-Which values from the Green Zone are appropriate to balance the issue?
V—Balance the issues and values balance
VI-Use the ROTH Format to write Thy Issues, Let Go Of, Be Thy Reality, Embrace and Thy Values
VII- Complete the ROTH Format.
VIII-List the values in the table as Primary, Secondary and Tertials

Homi: What about going through the sequence of these steps for Approach 1, using an example to illustrate and make it easier to understand.

Dr. Competence: Great idea, I can share Sue's story, her story illustrates an example of how we can go about using the ROTH-Approach 1. Sue was struggling with some issues that affected her life which she has delineated in her step 1 as follows:

I-Write a short story of your situation

Sue has written her issues in the following two paragraphs:

Sue is living with her adopted son who has Autism and lives in normal suburbia. Due to past bad experiences, she is worried about going out. She has developed a fear of meeting strangers and always stays at home. Her Life's Vision is to become a teacher specialised in the education of children who have developed Autism.

Sometimes the school invites parents to go to gatherings but she always avoids these gatherings. Sometimes when a small accident happens at school, she has a sudden panic attack and cannot make decisions, instead of being in control. When she discovers that it was a small matter that caused her to panic, she feels bad about herself for panicking. She is interested in pursuing a degree in the college nearby, but she has postponed it to next month after several postponements. With all her postponements, it is now two years since she made the decision to enrol.

Dr. Competence: The remaining steps, II to VII, that helped Sue to discover her values are as follows:

II-Underline the issues:

We need to identify the phrases or keywords that refer to the issues as listed in the RED ZONE in the ROTH that we might have.

Sue has underlined her issues as follows:

Sue is living with her adopted son who has Autism and lives in normal suburbia. Due to past bad experiences, <u>she is worried</u> about going out. She has developed a fear of meeting strangers and always stays at home. Her Life's Vision is to become a teacher specialised in the education of children who have developed Autism.

Sometimes the school invites parents to go to gatherings but she always avoids these gatherings. Sometimes when a small accident happens at school, she has a <u>sudden panic attack</u> and cannot make decisions, instead of being in control. When she discovers that it was a small matter that caused her to panic, she feels bad about herself for panicking. She is interested in pursuing a degree in the college nearby, but <u>she has postponed it to next month</u> after several postponements. With all her postponements, it is now two years since she made the decision to enrol.

The issues that Sue has referred to in the ROTH and written her issues as follows:

Fear of People, Anxiety, Panicky, Procrastination. These issues have created an imbalance in Sue's life as displayed underneath.

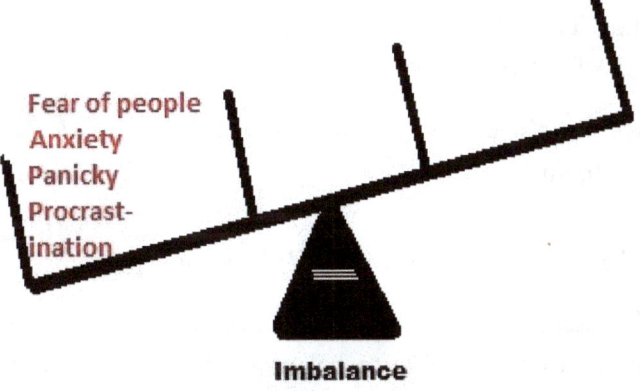

Figure 5.2 – Detailed issues causing imbalance

III- Find at what level the issues are located

Because there are some issues in Sue's case that are located at Level 1 of ROTH Framework, when we examine Sue's issues in the light of ROTH Framework, we quickly realise that her issues are located at, and relevant to, level one of the ROTH Framework. the first level, the "**Be Brave**" level or Stage.

IV-Then find in the Green Zone which values are appropriate to balance the situation

If Sue starts to look for these values, she would find them in Level one of the GREEN ZONE. While she would be reflecting on the values, she would realise that she can balance fear with courage.

As Sue also needs to stay calm when she experiences worries or anxiety, she may feel that she also needs to be strong, and to balance her procrastination she may think she also needs some more enthusiasm to do the things she wants to do in her life. These values are all listed in the GREEN ZONE at the LEVEL 1 or stage 1.

Hence, Sue's values are as follows: Courage, Calmness, Strength, and Enthusiasm.

V--Then make Issues and Values balance

In this step, Sue realises that by discovering and adopting these values, she is able to balance her life and resolve her issues. She can now start to practice them in her life. By doing so, she will realise that she can achieve the much-needed balance to continue her journey on the Vision Driven

Path to fulfil her Life's Vision. In this way Sue has balanced her issues and her values, as illustrated below:

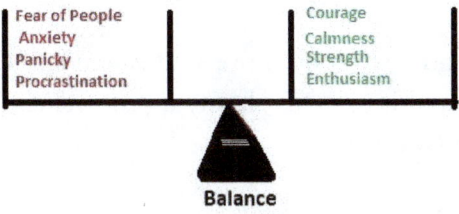

Figure 5.3 – Balancing Issues and Values

VI- Then use the ROTH format (a template comprised of five sections in three colours) refer below. Write the Issues, Let Go Of, Be Thy Reality, Embrace and Thy Values and values To sum up, we are using a ROTH Format, a template comprised of five sections in three colours, refer below. It is comprised of the Red Zone, Purple Zone, and Green Zone. For example, what Sue has achieved at the very start of her Journey on the Vision Driven Path and the result of working with the Rise of The Humans Framework (ROTH), as illustrated below in the ROTH Format (Red, Purple, and Green Zones):

Figure 5.4 – ROTH Format

THE RISE OF THE HUMANS

Homi: This is such a panorama, displaying information from addressing the issues to discovering the Values. Is this all Sue needed to do?

Dr. Competence: No, one more step is needed, the last step is important, and it is about classifying the values as Primary, Secondary and Tertials.

Homi: I have heard about Primary and Secondary, but what are the Tertials?

Dr. Competence: To understand this concept we need to learn about birds' wings, particularly the feathers birds require to fly high.

Homi: Why birds?

Dr. Competence: Because we use eagle wings as a metaphor to help humans create virtual wings, using values as virtual feathers. This approach enables human beings to fly to the heights of fulfilment virtually. In order to achieve that we need to help them create their virtual wings exactly like the wings of the birds like eagles, to make humans capable of flying virtually like birds.

Homi: This is amazing and unbelievable, but I believe it is possible for us as humans to fly to the heights of fulfilment, and for this I agree we need virtual wings like birds.

Dr. Competence: We are thus able to create new wings, the virtual wings, to fly like birds.

Homi: How?

Dr. Competence: By looking into the different types of feathers, and seeing the roles they play, based on their type, when they come together to work together as wings. I came this morning to create a slide, to show you how a bird's wings work, and how we can explain it.

Homi: That is even more exciting, let's go.

Dr. Competence: Okay Follow me,

We went through a couple of corridors, and we arrived in an average-size hall with a big screen at the front. When I entered, I noticed my voice echoed a little bit. Dr. Competence went to the front to present, and I sat watching the show.

Dr. Competence: Let's first focus on our feathers and our wings

Homi: We have been talking about rising high like birds, but we have not examined our wings. To fly high, we need our wings to be strong.

Dr. Competence: Exactly, our wings must be strongly built, and to rise as humans, we need wings like birds.

Homi: But of course, our wings are virtual and invisible.

Dr. Competence: Exactly! However, before we discuss our wings, it is better to examine the wings of birds.

Homi: Birds fly higher and higher using their wings.

Dr. Competence: Yes, look at this slide. As this slide shows, birds' wings are specially designed and covered with feathers as follows.

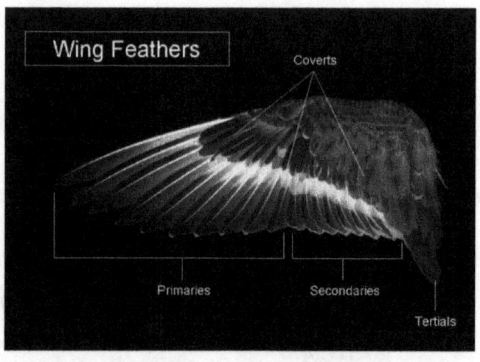

Figure 5.5 – Wing Feathers

Dr. Competence continued: The feathers have their functions and are grouped on that basis. They are either Primary Feathers, Secondary Feathers, Tertials and Coverts and each group has its own role to play in facilitating the flight of the birds.

Homi: So interesting, what are the Primary feathers and secondary feathers?

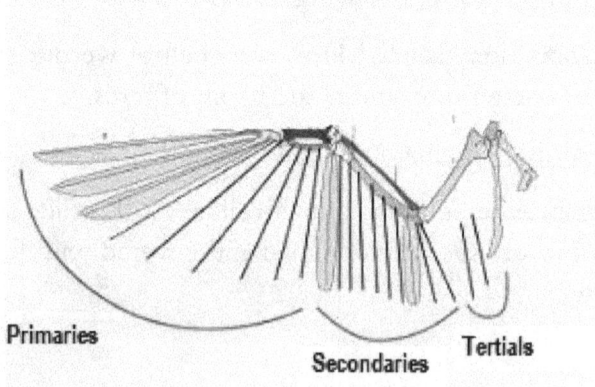

Figure 5.6 – Primary and Secondary Feathers

Dr. Competence: As the second slide also shows, Primary Feathers are the largest feathers that propel the bird through the air. Primary feathers are attached to the bones of the bird's hand. As air resists, these feathers propel the bird forward so that the bird can break the resistance and move forward.

Homi: How many Primary Feathers do the birds have?

Dr. Competence: Most birds have 9-10 Primary Feathers.

Homi: What about Secondary feathers, what do they do?

Dr. Competence: Secondary Feathers are to sustain the bird in the air giving it lift. These feathers are attached to the Ulna bob of the wings. There are 9 to 25 Secondary Feathers.

Homi: The slide shows that the birds also have Tertial feathers. What is their function?

Dr. Competence: These are the innermost feathers of the wing and are closer to the body of the bird attached to the

Homi: How many of these feathers do birds have?

Dr. Competence: They have between 3 and 4 Tertial feathers.

Homi: What about Coverts feathers, are they not one of the main feathers?

Dr. Competence: No, they are not. However, there are many of them. These Coverts are composed of 100s of small feathers that together with Tertials cover the Primary and Secondary feathers whenever the bird is not flying and is resting. While birds are flying, the Coverts protect the wings.

Homi: Why did you start with the structure of birds' wings this morning.

Dr. Competence: Because as you have guessed, the feathers represent the values that we hold in our hearts, although values are not visible like feathers, but they are grouped more or less like feathers on the bird's wings.

Homi: What do you mean by values grouped like feathers?

Dr. Competence: Like feathers, we require Primary, Secondary and Tertial Values to rise as humans.

Homi: What about Covert Values?

Dr. Competence: Well, the rest of the values that we don't list are coverts values that cover our virtual wings.

I remember focusing intensely on the last slide, reflecting on what Dr. Competence had said. I must have drifted off in thought because the next thing I heard was…

Dr. Competence: Are you with me? Homi, are you with me?

Homi: Yes, thank you. Very interesting, please continue.

Dr. Competence: Therefore, we need values that propel us forward, similar to a bird's Primary feathers as our invisible feathers. We can adopt our vision as one of our primary values to propel us forward. If so, it may be the most important one.

Homi: What about Secondary Values?

While Dr. Competence was looking at the slide, he mentioned:

Dr. Competence: "We need values that sustain us and lift us up as we rise, we also need these values to reach the heights of fulfilment".

Homi: Therefore, we need four types of values. Is that right?

Dr. Competence: Exactly, we need values that propel us to achieve, we need values that sustain us and maintain us to keep going so we do not give up, and as some values that lift us up, as well as values that protect us.

Homi: What about Tertial and covert Values?

Dr. Competence: Tertial and Covert feathers help the birds protect their flight feathers. Therefore, we also need some values that protect our primary and secondary values.

Homi: Which values propel us? Which values sustain us? Which values lift us up? And which values protect us?

Dr. Competence: Those are good questions, and we are going to find out all of these and answer these questions shortly.

Homi: Hence, we can learn that in our lives and pursuit of our vision, virtually, we also require values that propel us forward, values that sustain us and lift us up, and lastly, but not least, the values that protect us and our values.

Dr. Competence: If we are not propelled enough in pursuit of our vision, then we need to examine our values in that regard. If we start but do not sustain our progress, we need to check our secondary values, i.e. sustaining values

Homi: What about the values we have gone through and discovered in ROTH

Dr. Competence: We need to classify them into these categories and rank them in this manner.

Homi: Okay let's start to classify Sue's values.

Dr. Competence: Sue's values are classified as follows:

VII-Then list it in a table and classifying them into Primary, Secondary and Tertials

Classifying values into Primary, Secondary and Tertial in the following table.

Addressed Issues	Discovered Values	Primary Values Propelling	Secondary Values - Sustaining	Secondary Values - Lifting	Tertial and covert Protecting Values
Fear of people	Courage	Courage			
Anxiety	Calmness				Calmness
Panicky	Strength		Strength		
Procrastination	Enthusiasm			Enthusiasm	

Table 5.1 – Classifying Values

Homi: Sue's values were at the first stage or level of ROTH, what about other levels.

Dr. Competence: Well, other levels are similar to Sue's example, remember, we may not have issues at all levels, or we may have. However, if we don't, we need to learn ROTH-Approach 2 and decide whether we use Approach 1 or Approach 2 for each level of the Rise of The Humans Framework.

Homi: Do you mean like Approach 3- the Hybrid Approach.

Dr. Competence: Exactly, so let's have a look at ROTH-Approach 2.

ROTH- Approach 2

Step 1 – ROTH Values
Homi: What are ROTH values?

Dr. Competence: ROTH values are the values that are listed in the Green Zone of the Rise of The Humans Framework (ROTH). In ROTH-Approach 2:

Firstly, we need to classify these values at each of the levels or stages.

Secondly, we need to select four values at each stage.

Thirdly, we need to prioritise them.

Classifying ROTH Values

Homi: Okay, that is great. There are nine levels in ROTH; let's review and classify the stage one values listed in the Green Zone of the Rise of The Humans Framework (ROTH) in the previous chapter.

Dr. Competence: Okay, let us classify and rank ROTH Stage 1 values.

Homi: Great, but does everyone classify these values in a different way?

Dr. Competence: Yes, of course.

Homi: I interviewed Lilly, as you know, and I would like to classify based on that interview I carried out and the 20 pages of notes I made.

Dr. Competence: Fair enough; that is excellent. It would be a good example for illustration purposes.

Homi: Yes, it would be. Okay, the following classification into Primary, Secondary and Tertials is based on the interview with, and the data collected from, Lilly:

Courage
Steadfastness
Heroism
Calmness
Inner guidance
Trust
Insight
Conscious perception
Confidence
Enthusiasm
Spiritual Strength
Fortitude
Gratitude
Docility
Balance
Personal Development
Spirituality

Stage I – Be Brave	Primary Values Propelling	Secondary Values – Sustaining	Secondary Values – Lifting	Tertial and covert Protecting Values
Courage	Courage			
Trustfulness				Trustfulness

Spirituality				Spirituality
perception				Perception
Balance		Balance		
Inner Guidance				
Heroism	Heroism			
Calmness				Calmness
Guidance		Guidance		
Trust				Trust
Insight				Insight
Enthusiasm			Enthusiasm	
Steadfastness		Steadfastness		
Inner Guidance				Inner Guidance
Confidence	Confidence			
Fearlessness			Fearlessness	
Spiritual strength		Spiritual Strength		
Docility				Docility
Fortitude		Fortitude		
Gratitude		Gratitude		
Balance		Balance		
Personal Development	Personal Development			

Table 5.2 – Classifying Be Brave Values

Activity 1: You are required to classify your own.

Dr. Competence: Fantastic, great.

Homi: Does everyone classify the same way?

Dr. Competence: No, as I said, not at all, everyone will classify them differently. Everyone must reflect on each value, and decide to which column it belongs, which is a personal choice. Every individual may classify according to how they feel and perceive the values.

Homi: So, two individuals may come to two classifications.

Dr. Competence: Exactly, as different individuals are propelled by different values, everyone is different which is natural and okay.

Selecting ROTH Values

Homi: So, what do we do with these values?

Dr Competence: You can start to build your table by picking up one in each category, from each stage. For example, what would you like to pick from the above table's propelling or the primary values? Go to your heart and see which stands out for you in each category.

Homi: As an example, Lilly has chosen the following four values: Courage, Balance, Enthusiasm, and Spirituality.

The following table illustrates Lilly's chosen values and the allocating values to Primary, Secondary and Tertial at this level:

Stages	Primary Values Or Propelling Values	Secondary Values or Sustaining Values	Secondary Values or Lifting Values	Tertial Values Protecting Values
Be Brave	Courage	Balance	Enthusiasm	Spirituality

Table 5.3 –Lilly's Chosen Values for Level 1

Activity 2: You are required to complete your table.

Homi: So, at the end of this chapter you will have done nine analyses.

Dr. Competence: Exactly, and this forms part of our personal constitution; this is how we operate in life based on the values we believe in, and similarly, in the pursuit of our Life's Vision, this is the basis of how much we are able to rise as a human being, whilst we are sorting out life's issues and problems leading to the discovery of our personal values and growing as humans.

Homi: What, then, are our propelling values?

Dr. Competence: The propelling values are the values that propel us to achieve and fulfil our Life's Vision. For example, Achievement and Success.

Homi: Fair enough; what about Sustaining values?

Dr. Competence: Well, Sustaining Values are the ones that make us keep going and not giveing up, such as: Persistence, Perseverance.

Homi: And Lifting values?

Dr. Competence: Lifting values are secondary values that lift us up, cheer us up, make us rise in our mind and motivate us, such as: Joy, Enthusiasm, excitement.

Homi: What about protecting values?

Dr. Competence: Protecting Values: These values play a protecting role in our vision and goals, as well as protecting the rest of the values that we believe in, such as Trust, Inner Guidance.

Homi: Okay, do you suggest that we need to continue working with ROTH to deal with our issues and discover our values?

Dr. Competence: Yes, exactly; now let's start to look at the values at stage 2 – **"Be Certain"**

Homi: Okay, and this table illustrates Lilly's chosen values and their classification to Primary, Secondary, and Tertials at the "Be Certain" Stage (Stage 2):

Stage II - Be Certain	Primary Values Propelling	Secondary Values - Sustaining	Secondary Values - Lifting	Tertial and covert Protecting Values
Certainty		Certainty		
Trust in inner guidance				Trust in inner Guidance
Intuition				Intuition
Trust in own decisions				Trust in our decisions

Flexibility		Flexibility		
Clear Focus			Clear Focus	
Confidence	Confidence			
Inspiring			Inspiring	
Commitment		Commitment		
Energetic		Energetic		
Purposefulness	Purposefulness			
Good Judgement				Good Judgement
Obedience to Higher Self				Obedience to Higher Self
Vision	Vision		Vision	
Beliefs				Beliefs
Direction	Direction			
Self-trust				Self-Trust
Inspiration			Inspiration	
Energetic		Energetic		
Clarity				Clarity

Table 5.4 – Classifying Be Certain Values

Homi: How do we pick values from each stage?

Dr. Competence: Building a personal table of values must be based on addressing personal issues. We addressed them at each stage of the ROTH.

If we have no issues, then we need to pick the most important values, from each category of the ROTH framework, list them in the personal table, and allocate them as Primary, Secondary and Tertial. These are needed to create our Virtual Wings in the next section. Lilly's Table of Chosen Values is illustrated underneath:

| Be Brave | Courage | Balance | Enthusiasm | spirituality |
| Be Certain | Vision | Commitment | Clear Focus | Obedience to Higher Self |

Table 5.5 – Lilly's Chosen Values for 2 levels

Dr. Competence: When this table is completed, it forms part of a Personal Constitution.

Homi: What do you mean by Personal Constitution?

Dr. Competence: This becomes part of our Personal Constitution. Our personal constitution guides our decisions and actions in our life and our Life's Vision. Now continue for all remaining stages to come up with your own values as part of your personal constitution.

Stage III – Br Present	Primary Values Propelling	Secondary Values - Sustaining	Secondary Values - Lifting	Tertial and covert Protecting Values
Pray-fulness			Pray-fulness	
Forgiveness		Forgiveness		
Skilfulness			Skilfulness	
Creativity		Creativity		
Purposefulness	Purposefulness			
Taking action		Taking Action		
Mental Dexterity and sharpness			Mental Dexterity	

Excellent Perception				Excellent Perception
Assertiveness				Assertiveness
Vitality & Good Health	Good Health			
Longevity				Longevity
Excitement			Excitement	
Perseverance		Perseverance		
Command		Command		
Magnanimity and generosity				Magnanimity
Enthusiasm			Enthusiasm	
Action		Acting		
Embrace Opportunity			Embrace Opportunity	
Competence		Competence		
Confidence	Confidence			
Freedom			Freedom	
Inner Guidance				Inner Guidance

Table 5.6 – Classifying Be Present Values

Homi: Lilly has chosen these values: Good Health, Competence, Skilfulness, and Longevity, so her personal or chosen values table is updated as follows:

Stages	Primary Values Or Propelling Values	Secondary Values or Sustaining Values	Secondary Values or Lifting Values	Tertial values Protecting Values

Be Brave	Courage	Balance	Enthusiasm	spirituality
Be Certain	Vision	Commitment	Clear Focus	Obedience to Higher Self
Be Present	Good Health	Competence	Skilfulness	Longevity

Table 5.7 – Lilly's Chosen Values for 3 levels

Homi: How do we ensure that we are right in classifying the values as Primary, Secondary and Tertials?

Dr. Competence: The best way is to ask ourselves these questions to test our choice of values:

Ask yourself: What Propels Me and makes me Present?
Ask yourself: What Propels me and makes me Certain?
Ask yourself: What Propels me and makes me Brave?

Or ask in this manner and format: In the context of being social, does such a value propel me, sustain me, lift me or protect me?

Stage IV – Be Social	Primary Values Propelling	Secondary Values - Sustaining	Secondary Values - Lifting	Tertial an covert Protecting Values
Balance		Balance		
Understanding		Understanding		
Dignity				Dignity

Independence		Independence		
Patience				Patience
Sympathetic				Sympathetic
Empathy				Empathy
Friendliness	Friendliness		Friendliness	
Equality				Equality
Generosity			Generosity	
Prudence		Prudence		
Temperance				Temperance
Modesty		Modesty		
Purity				Purity
Clemency				Clemency
Kindness			Kindness	
Love	Love		Love	
Patience		patience		
Moderation				Moderation
Courtesy		Courtesy		
Affability	Affability			
Tolerance		Tolerance		
Compassion				Compassion
Sociable				Sociable

Table 5.8 – Classifying Be Social Values

Stages	Primary Values Or Propelling Values	Secondary Values or Sustaining Values	Secondary Values or Lifting Values	Tertial values Protecting Values
Be Brave	Courage	Balance	Enthusiasm	spirituality
Be Certain	Vision	Commitment	Clear Focus	Obedience to Higher Self
Be Present	Good Health	Competence	Skilfulness	Longevity
Be Social	Love	Understanding	Generosity	Sociable

Table 5.9 –Lilly's Chosen Values for 4 levels

Homi: How do we go about this activity?

Dr. Competence: Just be Genuine, and don't make it up. We need to be honest to ourselves.

Homi: How do we make it genuine?

Dr. Competence: Ask: What am I? Who am I? Be honest and genuine as you are on your way to discovering your personal set of values that you run in your life which are the basis of your decisions and actions; it is a source of your inspiration, a component of your Personal Constitution that will reveal who you are to yourself. You want to know who you are, don't you?

Homi: Yes, of course

Dr. Competence: Okay, so ask questions like the following.

What primary value makes me feel great and good about Being Social?
What secondary value makes me feel great and good about Being Social?
What Lifting value makes me feel great and good about Being Social
What Protecting value makes me feel great and good about Being Social?

For the remaining stages from Be Open to Be Global you need to continue the approach, asking similar questions in order to allocate the values and then choose your values for each level. Lilly's remaining stages or levels are as follows:

Stage V – Be Open	Primary Values Propelling	Secondary Values – Sustaining	Secondary Values – Lifting	Tertial and covert Protecting Values
Honesty				Honesty
Openness		Openness		
Inner Joy			Inner Joy	
Harmony		Harmony		
Optimism			Optimism	
Awareness of one's needs		Awareness of one's needs		
Truthfulness				Truthfulness
Steadfastness		Steadfastness		
Taking the Last step	Taking the Last step			
Generosity			Generosity	
Good will				Good will
Love	Love			

Inner Harmony		Inner Harmony		
Understanding		Understanding		
Peacefulness			Peacefulness	
Sincerity				Sincerity
Foresight				Foresight
Radiating Good Will			Radiating Good Will	
Warm Heartedness			Warm Heartedness	

Table 5.10 – Classifying Be Open Values

Stage VI – Be Accepting	Primary Values Propelling	Secondary Values – Sustaining	Secondary Values – Lifting	Tertial and covert Protecting Values
Confidence	Confidence			
Success	Success			
Self-Acceptance			Self-Acceptance	
Self-worth				Self-worth
Endurance		Endurance		
Constructiveness				Constructiveness
Creativity	Creativity			
Joyfulness			Joyfulness	
Believing in your self		Believing in your self		

Responsibility		Responsibility		
Connect to higher self			Connect to higher self	
Commitment		Commitment		
Skilfulness		Skilfulness		
Strength			Strength	
Loyalty		Loyalty		
Prosperity	Prosperity			

Table 5.11 – Classifying Be Accepting Values

Stage VII – Be Serving	Primary Values Propelling	Secondary Values –Sustaining	Secondary Values - Lifting	Tertial and covert Protecting Values
Professionalism		Professionalism		
Wisdom				Wisdom
Justice				Justice
Service			Service	
Helpfulness				Helpfulness
Respect			Respect	
Tolerance		Tolerance		
Meekness		Meekness		
Flexibility		Flexibility		
Attentiveness	Attentiveness			
Spontaneity				Spontaneity
Lenience		Lenience		
Empathy				Empathy
Mental Acuity				Mental Acuity
Understanding		Understanding		

Enthusiasm			Enthusiasm	
Inspiring			Inspiring	
Integrity				Integrity
Justice				Justice
Patience		Patience		
Loving	Loving			
Rule of law				Rule of law

Table 5.12 – Classifying Be Serving Values

Stage VIII – Be Visionary	Primary Values Propelling	Secondary Values –Sustaining	Secondary Values - Lifting	Tertial and covert Protecting Values
Vision	Vision			
Mastery		Mastery		
Fulfilment			Fulfilment	
Achievement	Achievement			
Success	Success			
Passion			Passion	
Dreams			Dreams	
Driven		Driven		
Upliftment			Upliftment	
Circumspection		Circumspection		
Industriousness		Industriousness		
Diligence				Diligence
Orderliness				Orderliness
Becoming	Becoming			
Purposeful	Purposeful			
Realisation				Realisation
Greatness			Greatness	
Highest Aspiration			Highest Aspiration	
Blessed				Blessed
Glorious			Glorious	

| | | | Enlighted | |
| | | | Exemplar | |

Table 5.13– Classifying Be Visionary Values

Stage IX – Be Global, World Embracing	Primary Values Propelling	Secondary Values - Sustaining	Secondary Values - Lifting	Tertial and covert Protecting Values
Unity		Unity		
Oneness	Oneness		Oneness	
Humanity				Humanity
Unitedness				Unitedness
Globalism			Globalism	
One World, One Family	One world, One family			
One Human Race	One Human Race			
Unity in Diversity		Unity in Diversity		
Global Community				Global Community
Global Market				Global Market
Internationalis	Internationalism			
Earth as one home			Earth as one home	
Extraordinaires			Extraordinaires	
World Citizenship				World Citizenship
Togetherness		Togetherness		

Spirit of oneness	Spirit of oneness			
Multiculturalism				Multiculturalism
Be one			Be One	
One World Family				One World Family
Multicultural				Multicultural
Global		Global		
World Citizenship			World Citizenship	

Table 5.14– Classifying Be Global Values

Homi: Okay, what do we need next?

Dr. Competence: Next, we need to look at the final table and reflect to determine whether we cherish any values in our hearts that we would like to add to the table. If so, that is fine; make sure to add those values as "Added Values".

Homi: What about vision as a value, our Life's Vision?

Dr. Competence: If we have not selected vision as one of our values so far but have identified it as one of our values, we can add it now at this stage.

Homi: What do we do if we have several values to add?

Dr. Competence: That is fine, too; add those values to the last row of the table. For example, Lilly has chosen the following values to add to her table:

| X – Added Values | Money | Wealth | Fame | Persistence |

Table 5.15: Added Values

Lilly's complete Table of Values is as follows:

Stages	Primary Values Or Propelling Values	Secondary Values or Sustaining Values	Secondary Values or Lifting Values	Tertial values Protecting Values
I – Be Brave	Courage	Balance	Enthusiasm	spirituality
II – Be Certain	Vision	Commitment	Clear Focus	Obedience to Higher Self
III – Be Present	Good Health	Competence	Skilfulness	Longevity
IV – Be Social	Love	Understanding	Generosity	Sociable
V – Be Open	Taking the last step	Inner Harmony	Inner Joy	Sincerity
VI – Be Accepting	Success	Endurance	Strength	Self-Worth
VII – Be Serving	Loving	Flexibility	Service	Integrity
VIII – Be Visionary	Achievement	Driven	Fulfilment	Orderliness

IX – Be Global	Internationalism	Unity	Globalism	Global Market
X –	Money	Wealth	Fame	Persistenc

Table 5.16 Lilly's Complete Chosen Values

Prioritising the Values

Homi: Okay, what is the next step after we have added the extra values?

Dr. Competence: We only need to work on the four columns. First, we need to prioritise the Primary values, from the most important to the least important, by placing a representative number between 1 and 10 next to the Values in this column.

Homi: What about the Secondary Values?

Dr. Competence: We need to choose ten values from columns 2 and 3 because we need to choose 10 Secondary Values out of the twenty Values listed in those columns. Again, we will indicate their priority level by placing a number between 1 and 10 next to each of these Values as follows (in the example below):

Homi: What about the Tertial Values?

Dr. Competence: We need to find the two most important values. The following table illustrates the result of Lilly's choice of Value rankings. She has prioritised her Values as follows:

Primary Values Or Propelling Values	Secondary Values or Sustaining Values	Secondary Values or Lifting Values	Tertial values Protecting Values
7-Courage	1-Balance	10-Enthusiasm	spirituality
1-Vision	Commitment	6-Clear Focus	2-Obedience to Higher Self
2-Good Health	5-Competence	Skilfulness	1-Longevity
8-Love	Understanding	Generosity	Sociable
10-Taking the last step	2-Inner Harmony	Inner Joy	Sincerity
3-Success	Endurance	Strength	Self-Worth
9-Loving	3-Flexibility	8-Service	Integrity
4-Achievement	Driven	9-Fulfilment	Orderliness
6-Internationalism	4-Unity	7-Globalism	Global Market
5-Money	Wealth	Fame	Persistence

Table 5.17 - Lilly's Prioritised Values

The Rise of The Humans Framework – Hybrid Approach

In the Hybrid Approach you work with both approaches. For example, suppose you have issues at some Level of the ROTH Framework. In that case, you can discover your values by using your issues to guide you to the opposing values. Firstly, let's assume your problems are at the Be Brave and Be Present Levels/Stages. For these two Levels, you use Approach 1. Next, for the other Stages, you would use Approach 2, where you classify the values according to your liking and choose the values as you wish to come up with four values at each level. When you have forty values, then choose 10 values for Primary, 10 for Secondary Values and 2 Tertial Values.

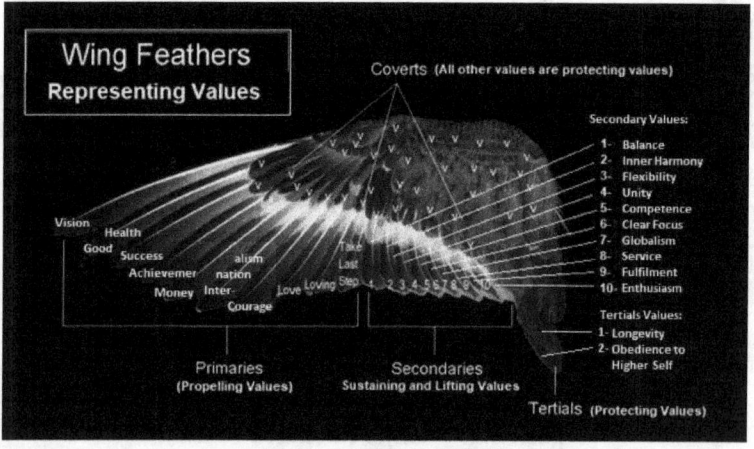

Figure 5.7 – Lilly's Wings representing her values

Creating Our Virtual Wings

After we have completed ranking our selected values, we are ready to create our virtual wings composed of Primaries, Secondaries and Tertials. The following example illustrates

Lilly's virtual wings and the combination of Primary, Secondary and Tertial feathers in her wings:

In this way, we can construct our wings as illustrated above. Our other wing is the replica and, therefore, the mirror image of the wing we have already built. The power that emanates from using these two wings to fly to the heights of fulfilment is beyond our imagination. When we find our genuine values to construct our own wings, we feel amazing and exponentially empowered.

Activity: You are required to create your wings as you need them to rise to the heights of fulfilment of your vision.

To summarise:
In the previous exercise above, you learned how to create your wings. Here I will summarise the process: Utilising the Rise of The Humans Framework (ROTH), we virtually discovered our Primary, Secondary, Tertial and Covert values. We need to have 10 propelling empowering values, which are our Primaries. We also need to have ten Secondary Values comprising Sustaining and Lifting Values. In addition, we need two or three Tertial Values that are protecting values. Any other values we have left will be our Covert Values which are also protecting.

Our Primary values also form part of our Core Values. These values propel us forward; they have the empowering, energising effect that makes us advance. Therefore, when we rank or prioritise them, we end up having one value at the top of the primary values. This value has the most propelling effect of all the Primary Values and could be anything, including vision. That said, be careful how you prioritise your Primary Values or Core Values.

Rise of The Humans Framework – ROTH-Approach 3, the Hybrid Approach

In the Hybrid Approach, you work with both approaches. You use Approach 1 when you have issues and Approach 2 when you don't. For example, if you have issues at any level of ROTH, you discover your values by using the issue as a guide to finding the opposing values. In the other stages, when you do not have any issues, you use Approach 2.

Chapter 6
Discovering your Life's Vision and Personal Constitution

> *"Your vision will become clear only when you look into your heart. Who looks outside, dreams, who looks inside, awakens."*
> - Carl Jung

> *"The clearer you are about what you want, the less time you waste chasing dead-ends and the faster you make your life goals happen."*
> - Mark Anastasi (Laptop Millionaire)

After all the knowledge we gained from the previous chapters (Chapters 4 and 5) regarding our life's values, it is essential to become clear about what our visions are. The question is: "How can we become certain about our vision, our Life's Vision?' So far, we have reflected on what we love, our talents, and our values as individuals. So, by getting to this point in the book, we might already have a very good idea of what our vision could be. Your idea might be right, or you may need to get confirmation by meditating on your Life's Vision, or as you will have noticed in the story of Lilly, sometimes it takes time to discover your true Life's Vision.

The following Wednesday, just before lunch, as I was doing some writing, I realised that one more thing could be that our mind still needs some clarity. So, I thought to call Dr.

Competence to see if he is available to discuss the problem at his home.

Homi: Hello Dr. Competence: good morning; this is Homi

Dr. Competence: Yes, I know your voice well; what's up? How are you doing with the writing? Any progress?

Homi: Yes, it is still ongoing, but I have some lingering thoughts and intriguing questions about how we become certain and clear of our vision.

Dr. Competence: Well, of course there are ways to clear the mind to become sure about our vision.

Homi: Yes, I agree, but what is the best approach?

Dr. Competence: So, would you like to come up for a cup of tea?

Homi: That is what I was thinking.

Dr. Competence: If that is what you were thinking, why not? See you soon; it is sunny today, the weather is friendly, and I am home, come on.

Homi: Okay, see you in an hour

On my way to see Dr. Competence at his residence, I was excitedly looking forward to seeing the rivers and the boats from his balcony.

I arrived and was immediately made to feel welcome again. Dr. Competence already made the tea ready. When I arrived, he showed me a new room I had not seen before. He said, "I want to show you something, so follow me". He went in the opposite direction to where the kitchen was and straight towards the end of that corridor on the left. He opened a door and asked me to enter the room. It was a small cinema with eight chairs like the real cinema chairs.

Homi: Wow! Do you watch movies here?

Dr. Competence: Yes, sometimes, I don't watch TV shows, only the news. But sometimes I watch good movies that are interesting, documentaries and other movies once a week.

Then we went to his library again, and he poured me some tea.

Dr. Competence: When we are together, something magical happens, and we become more explicit about the new chapters you are writing.

Homi: I feel the same; it just flows and starts to shape up as we start the conversation about any topic.

Dr. Competence: Let's start and let the conversation flow

While sipping his tea, Homi began by saying.

Homi: Okay, that sounds great. In the previous chapter, we explored our talents, what we love to do, and how to work with the Rise of The Humans Framework to discover our values. Now, we want to be as straightforward as possible about what our vision is.

Homi: What we are going to discuss in this Chapter.

Dr. Competence: In this chapter, we will get even more precise about our visions by going through several clarification activities, which include using the following tools:

- A Venn Diagram to clarify.
- The Arrow of Vision - By going through the components required to create the arrow of vision, we become clearer about our vision.
- The Four Quadrants - By understanding Vision, goals, and the relationship between them, we become clearer about our vision, because our goals are not our vision or vice versa.
- Understanding the Tree of Vision – This understanding helps us to grasp the relationships of the components of knowledge, values, goals, focus and strategies.
- The Four levels of competence provide a transparent view of where we are.

I - Using a Venn Diagram to clarify our Life's Vision

Homi: What is a Venn Diagram and what is its function?

Dr. Competence: Venn diagrams illustrate how ideas overlap, by using circles, showing the logical relationship between two or more sets of ideas or concepts. For example, in Chapters 4 and 5, we went through the ROTH Framework to discover our values. The ROTH Framework three components, i.e. Let go of, Be, and Embrace. The following Venn Diagram illustrates these three components of the ROTH Framework:

Discovering your Life's Vision and Personal Constitution

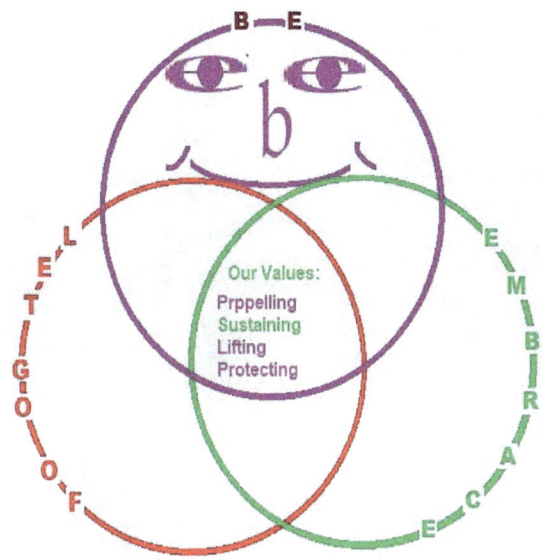

Figure 6.1 – Venn diagram showing Let Go of, Embrace and Be

Dr. Competence: In the previous chapters, we discovered what we love to do and made a list: we found what our talents are and made a list, and what our values are and made a list. These three lists are essential to help us find, in a heuristic way, our Life's Vision. The way to clarify with Venn diagrams is by bringing in the mix of the three ideas next to each other and letting them overlap.

Homi: Exactly; overlapping the concepts of what we love to do, our talents and our values inspire us and guide us to our Life's Vison.

Dr. Competence: Now, let us consider these three lists in a Venn diagram to understand them more clearly. This process/activity inspires us about our Life's Vision, although we may have some idea by now.

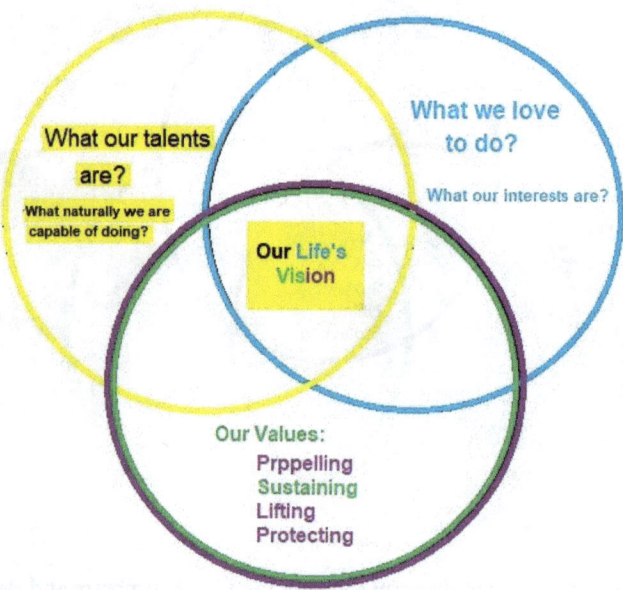

Figure 6.2 – Venn diagram showing what we love to, our talents and our values

Homi: Yes, I can clearly see relationship between these three concepts. Why is the circle for values in Green and Purple?

Dr. Competence: The two circles represent the Green Zone and the Purple Zone in the ROTH Framework.

Homi: Can you provide an example how the Venn Diagram works?

Dr. Competence: Yes, of course. The best example is Lilly's case. As you have interviewed Lilly, tell me what she loves to do.

Homi: Lilly told me she loves both Dancing and Tai Chi.

Dr. Competence: And what about her talents?

Discovering your Life's Vision and Personal Constitution

Homi: Her talents are Calligraphy, Teaching, Dance, Body movement and Photography.

Dr. Competence: Well, we also discovered her values based on the interview with her and the ROTH Framework findings.

Homi: Yes.

Dr. Competence: The following Venn Diagram condenses Lilly's data and her vision

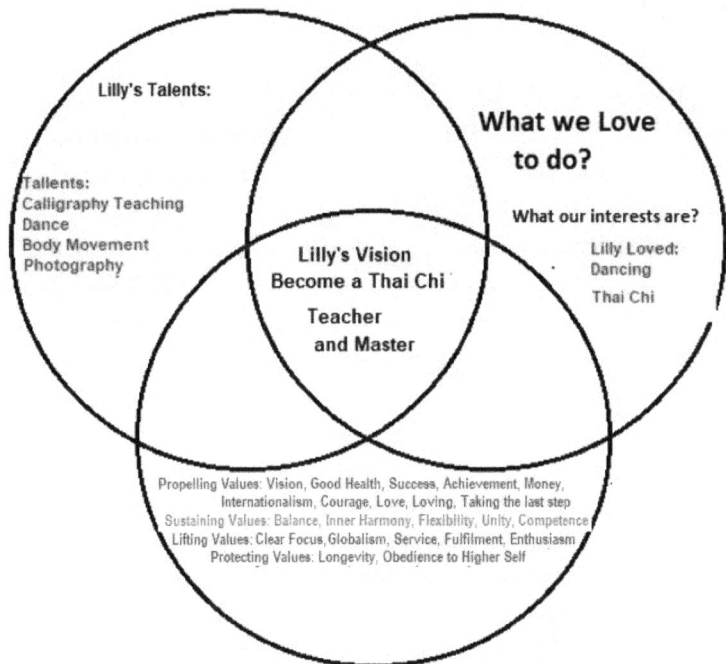

Figure 6.3 – Lilly's Venn Diagram

Homi: How can we explain Lilly's Venn Diagram - How and why she has come to have such a vision?

Dr. Competence: Simple. Looking at her values, you will realise that the top Propelling Value or Primary Value/s after the vision is "Good Health", right?

Homi: Right.

Dr. Competence: Okay, if you examine her talents, you will realise she has listed body movement, that is for health too.

Homi: Fair enough.

Dr. Competence: If we check what she loves to do, you have also found out that she loves dancing and Tai Chi, for Good Health.

Homi: Do you mean there is a common denominator that her Venn Diagram is revealing?

Dr. Competence: Exactly! as the following Venn Diagram illustrates:

Discovering your Life's Vision and Personal Constitution

Figure 6.4 – Illustrating how what we love to do, our talents and values inter-relate to our vision

Homi: In other words, Lilly is fulfilling her top value, i.e., "Good Health", which she believes to be vital for a fulfilling life. The top value is the driving force that empowers her to fulfil her Life's Vision

Dr. Competence: Exactly

Homi: But I thought that her top value is her Vision and her next top value after her Vision is "Good Health"

Dr. Competence: In fact, the first top five values are all strong values. However, if you pick your first value to be your vision, the next value supporting your vision is just as powerful. In Lilly's case, that Value is "Good Health". All these values can also be listed as your Personal Constitution plus your talents and what you love to do.

Homi: So, the Venn Diagram above for Lilly also represents Lilly's Personal Constitution?

Dr. Competence: Exactly, as illustrated in Lilly's Personal Constitution which follows:

Lilly's Personal Constitution

Name: Lilly		Life's Vision: Become a Thai Chi Teacher and Promoter	
What are your Talents and Gifts		What you love to do	
• Calligraphy • Dance • Body Movement • Photography		• Dancing • Thai Chi	
Your Propelling Values	Your Sustaining Values	Your Lifting Values	Your Protecting Values
1. Vision, 2. Good Health, 3. Success, 4. Achievement, 5. Money, 6. Internationalism, 7. Courage, 8. Love, 9. Loving, 10. Taking the last step	1. Balance, 2. Inner Harmony, 3. Flexibility, 4. Unity, 5. Competence	1. Clear Focus, 2. Globalism, 3. Service, 4. Fulfilment, 5. Enthusiasm	1. Longevity, 2. Obedience to Higher Self

Table 6.1 – Lilly's Personal Constitution

Activity: In the following Venn Diagram write your Talents. What you love to do, Your Values and Your Vision.

Discovering your Life's Vision and Personal Constitution

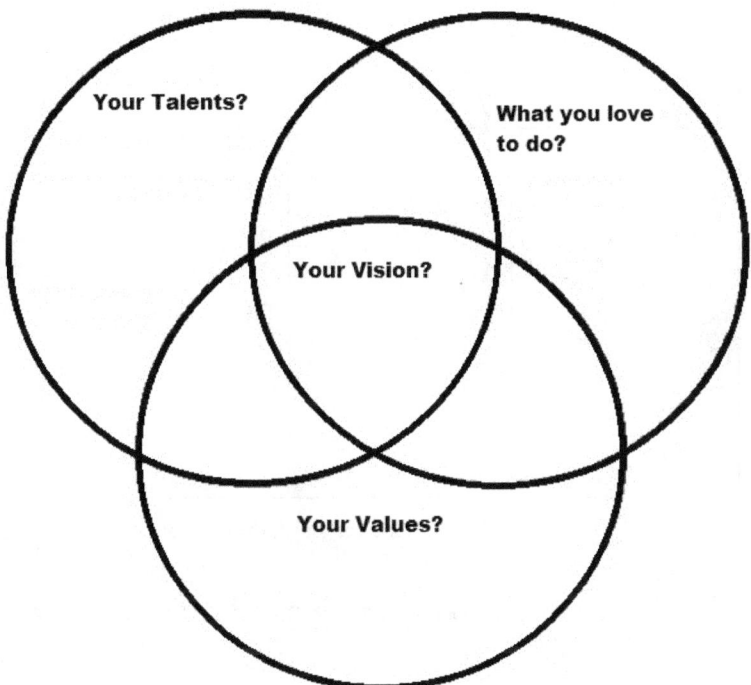

Figure 6.5 – Blank Venn diagram

Activity: Create your Personal Constitution, complete the following form and write your Talents, what you love to do, your values and your Life's Vision.

Personal Constitution

Name:	Life's Vision:
What are your Talents and Gifts	What you love to do
1- 2- 3- 4- 5	1- 2- 3- 4- 5-

Your Propelling Values	Your Sustaining Values	Your Lifting Values	Your Protecting Values
1- 2- 3- 4- 5- 6- 7- 8- 9- 10	1- 2- 3- 4- 5-	1- 2- 3- 4- 5-	1- 2-

Table 6.2 – Blank Personal Constitution

II – Creating and constructing our Arrow of Vision –

Homi: We learned about Venn diagrams and how to clarify our Life's Vision by putting the three circles together and finding the overlap of What We Love, Our Talents and Our Values. Do we achieve the same thing with the Arrow of Vision?

Dr. Competence: No, an arrow gives us a sense of direction. It clarifies the sense of direction that our vision conveys to us whilst bringing in the three elemental relationships from the Venn Diagram. The Arrow of Vision is one step further than the Venn Diagram because it displays the direction we are heading towards, in addition. It is our Life's Vision at the point of the **Arrow of Vision** that defines our Life's Direction. It is fuelled by a set of values that we hold, empowered by what we love, and assisted by our talents and natural gifts, as

Discovering your Life's Vision and Personal Constitution

in the example below. Having a clear direction, we are better off when confronted with a decision.

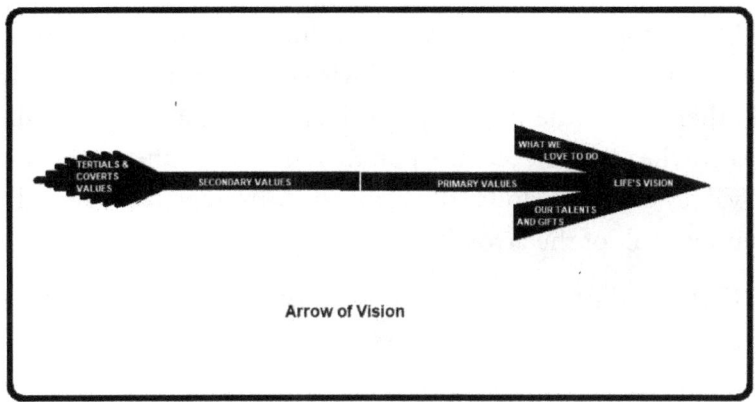

Figure 6.6 – Arrow of Vision

Homi: Can you clarify what you mean by that?

Dr. Competence: You see, everyone constantly makes decisions and takes action. In this way, we grow and become more experienced in this life. Our vision specifies our direction, guiding us to be clear on our choices and actions.

Homi: Do you think our life's purpose is to grow? Then how do we grow?

Dr. Competence: We are here in this life to grow which needs discovering our vision. Our vision gives us our direction. Our vision is born of our talents as a father, what we love as a mother, and is guided by our most important values.

Homi: How are these represented on the Arrow of Vision?

Dr. Competence: What you love to do, your highest value, and your gifts and talents form the arrowhead.

Homi: What about the shaft and fletching? Which values do they represent in this analogy?

Dr. Competence: The Primary Value that propels the arrow starts in the arrowhead aligned with the shaft at the centre. In other words, the highest propelling value is at the tip of the arrowhead at the centre point. The rest of the propelling values continue down the arrow and are represented by the upper half of the arrow's shaft.

Homi: What about the Secondary Values comprised of Sustaining and Lifting Values?

Dr. Competence: The Values listed on the shaft are Primary, Secondary and Tertial values. Our Core Values are the primary values that drive our arrow of vision.

Homi: What about the Secondary Values and Tertials?

Dr. Competence: These values are in the lower part of the shaft and fletching.

III-The Four Goal-Vision Quadrants

Homi: How can we become clear about our Life's Vision?

Dr. Competence: We need to understand that our goals are our goals and our Life's Vision is our Life's Vision. In other words, we need to differentiate between our goals and our Life's Vision and between High Achievers and Low Achievers, which is explained in the goals and vision quadrants below.

Homi: One example is to think of an orange tree. An orange tree's vision is to reach the point of becoming, which means being able to produce oranges. The orange tree has oranges and leaves that benefits the tree as part of growing oranges.

Discovering your Life's Vision and Personal Constitution

For example, due to of Gandhi's Vision Tree, some people started to follow him, and government officials gradually changed their behaviour along the way. These benefits if not accrued to Gandhi, the fruit of his efforts might not have been produced. Therefore, benefits are like the leaves and need to appear before flowering and fruition occur. They are the signs that the fruit is on the way and needs the leaves to benefit from the sun. As more benefits were accrued to Gandhi, more leaves appeared on Gandhi's Vision Tree. They empowered the tree with more oxygen, and the flowers bloomed.

Dr. Competence: Blooming flowers indicate that the opposing forces are ready to reconcile. Differences are resolved, and the parties are coming together in unity. The contradictory forces in nature must unite for the fruit to appear. Similarly, in terms of Gandhi's Vision tree, there were a few; the British resisting, the people in jail, the government officials still in charge, demonstrators in danger, and the marches were ongoing.

Homi: So, blooming flowers show opposing forces are coming together, and reconciling. Like the tree that brings the unity of the female and male via the vehicle of flowering, Gandhi's vision tree started to bloom. The blooming led to fruition, that was the purpose.

Dr. Competence: When this happens, it is a sign that the appearance of the fruit is near. In Gandhi's case, the Government announced Independence and concluded British rule in India and freedom was on the horizon.

Homi: In other words, blooming for the Tree of Vision means unity for the tree to bear fruit is happening. This flowering leads to fruition, and the fruit is the purpose. So, what started in the root a while ago now appears as flowers, making the fruit come true. Therefore, fruit from the start was in the seed of vision. Now, check the following four quadrants:

	No Vision	Have Vision	
Have Goals	G - Moderate Achievers	GV - High Achievers	Have Goals
No Goals	Low Achievers	V - Moderate Achievers	No Goals

Table 6.3 – Goals Vision Quadrants

We now go through the Four Quadrants and discuss each of the quadrants:

1 – Low Achievers - Have No Goal & Have No Vision

If we have no goal and no vision, we do not have a target to aim at. We live, just eating and sleeping. If we work, we just spend the money earned on food and necessities and we are not interested in setting goals, achieving goals, discovering our vision, or fulfilling it.

Since vision gives us direction, we become as Maxwell Maltz put it, a "servo-mechanism". It means that by finding our Life's Vision and setting goals to fulfil it, we become like self-aiming missiles steering our way to its fulfilment. It becomes "our built-in servo-mechanism" functioning within us in the right direction to achieve goals or make correct responses to the environment to fulfil our Life's Vision. Without our Life

Discovering your Life's Vision and Personal Constitution

Vision and goals, we become directionless. Goals are necessary stepping stones to our Life's Vision.

2 – G-Moderate Achiever - Have Goal & but No Vision

Some people may set goals, but they have no Life Vision. They have no long-term direction in life although settings goals might give them a temporary direction. After the goal is achieved, they are lost again, until they set new goals. In other words, they have yet to have an ultimate vision, a direction. They may feel great upon achieving of their goals, but it is short-lived. After some laps of time, they may think, "when I set this goal, I was very excited, but after I have achieved it I don't feel happy and I don't know why?

The reason is that they need to see the goals as stepping stones that bring them one step closer to the fulfilment of their Life's Vision.

3 – Have No Goal & But have Vision

This quadrant represents those people who have discovered their vision but have set no goals. Individuals in this group may have found their vision, which is excellent, but goals are still being determined. Or, they may regard their vision as a long-term goal and have yet to plan several goals as stepping stones leading to their Life's Vision. Their vision looks like a ladder without rungs to go step by step to the top.

4 – High Achievers - Have Goals and Have a Vision

This quadrant is the best of all four. Individuals in this quadrant are "High Achievers" in all fields, from science to social, from commerce to technology, and from economics to politics, they have achieved highly in every area. Some achieved higher levels of wealth, but all achieved fame in their own right. Gandhi was a High Achiever and his goals were not his vision. His goals, like stepping stones, helped his vision to materialize and come true. Of course, he set his goals based on his strategies aiming to fulfil his vision.

People in this quadrant a have vision, but they also have goals. The ladder is much more beautiful and elegant, and it is possible to get to the top because it has rungs. We like to climb this ladder to rise higher and higher. People feel they have wings, and rising as humans, higher and higher. This is a fabulous quadrant to be in.

By now, you have either discovered your life vision or you may have a firm idea of your Life's Vision and goals. So, it is time to articulate your vision and explain in simple words what your vision and goals are.

Year	List Your Goals	Articulate Your Vision
......	Goal	In a few lines articulate your life's vision underneath:
......	Goal	....
......	Goal	....
......	Goal	....
......	Goal	....
......	Goal	....
......	Goal	....
......	Goal	....
......	Goal	....
......	Goal	....

Table 6.4 – Your Goals and Vision

Discovering your Life's Vision and Personal Constitution

IV-Mastery in understanding Vision tree

To develop mastery of our Life's Vision we need to learn from masters who already fulfilled their Life's Vision, and, in this book, we call them Masters of Vision, a term I have coined for Visionaries. We refer to a few of the Masters of Vision, such as Helen Keller, Gandhi, Jack Ma, Steve Jobs and Mark Zuckerberg. Also, Lilly's case is introduced as an illustrating example throughout the book. We can learn from these illustrations to formulate our own Life's Vision. In addition, we can learn from Lilly's case to do the activities presented in the text. You can compare these examples with your own life and discover the lessons you need to learn.

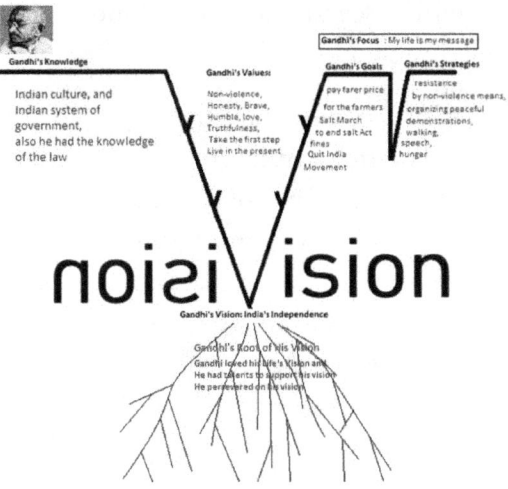

Figure 6.7 – Gandhi's Vision Tree

One of the Masters of Vision was Gandhi. When we examine Gandhi's Tree of Vision, we realise that he had vast knowledge which he gained during his life. Just check out the list of topics Gandhi learned and had in his repertoire of knowledge. Pay attention to the number of goals he set and achieved, although, we listed just a few of his important goals. First, his goals were not his vision, this was discussed in the previous section of this chapter. His goals helped his vision materialise. Of course, he set his goals in congruence with his strategies aimed at fulfilling of his vision. So, our goals need to be within our strategy. Without formulating proper strategies, we should not set goals. Also, we must ensure that our goals are congruent with our vision. In other words, our goals must be both congruent with our vision and strategies.

Now, when we examine Lilly's teacher, we realise that he also had excellent knowledge, in his case it was about Tai Chi, the origins of Tai Chi, Tai Chi Philosophy, etc., and he also practised Tai Chi regularly. He ran it as a business, his focus had been to ascend unceasingly, and he had his goals, and his Life's Vision.

The outcomes of our vision are the fruits our tree of vision tree produces. The tree's fruits are served to humanity, who partake of the fruit. The fruits of our endeavours are provided as services and products we can offer our customers, clients, and users. Therefore, it is clear that our purpose in pursuing our Life's Vision is to produce some services or products. Of course, to produce fruits the tree needs to use the energy to be empowered. The leaves appear on the tree to facilitate using the Sun's energy. Social network members, followers and fans are some examples of leaves on the tree of vision. The tree gets some benefits from the leaves to produce fruits. Our life's purpose is the fruits produced by the Vision Tree.

While in Steve Jobs' Tree of Vision we are able to see the range of his knowledge, as well as the goals he had.

Discovering your Life's Vision and Personal Constitution

Your love and passion water the root of the Tree of Vision. You water it for what you love to do and your passion for the talents you have. The water absorbed by the root travels through the stems to branches and leaves. Your love and passion reach to entire Tree of Vision and become verdant leading to fruition.

Activity: Create your own Vision Tree

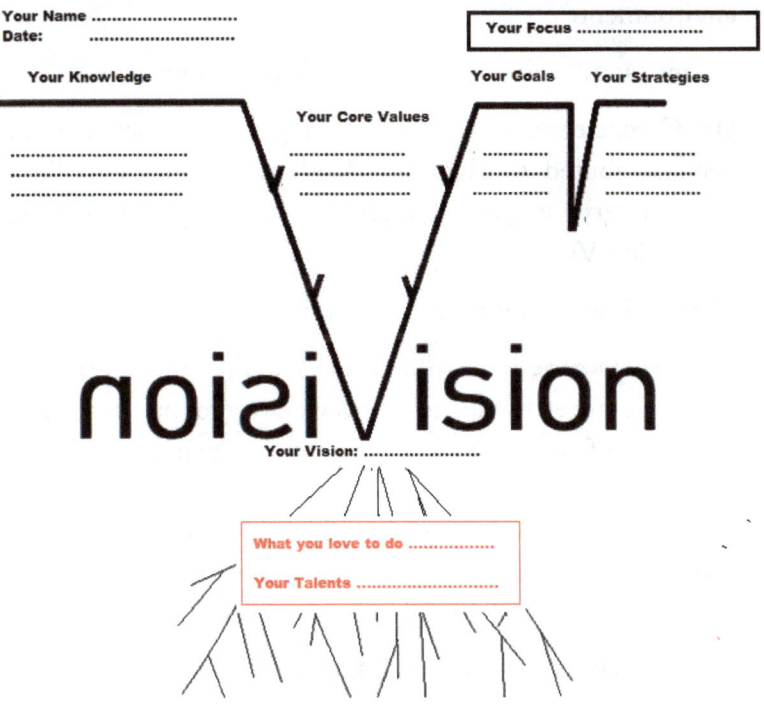

Figure 6.8 – Create your Vision Tree

V-Four levels of Visional Competence

Homi: We learned that to be a High Achiever we need, Goals and Vision. In the four levels of competence, we need to become masters of our vision by understanding and progressing to become better and better until we are satisfied with our competence and abilities.

Dr. Competence: Those who are masters of vision have achieved unconscious competence and can function without consciously controlling all their actions. They have developed the knowledge of their Life's Vision and environment.

Homi: Does everyone goes through these four stages?

Dr. Competence: Yes, these four stages of competence have been attributed to Abraham Maslow (Hughes and Read, 2012). Everyone goes through these four stages of mastering their Life's Vision.

Homi: How does it work?

Dr. Competence: In terms of understanding, these four stages of competence, it explains how we are moving from being unaware of our Life's Vision to achieving mastery in articulating, planning, and setting congruent goals towards its fulfilment. The following table summarises the four stages of competence in relation to mastery of our Life's Vision.

Four levels of Visional Competence

Unconscious Incompetence
We are not aware of our Life's Vision and its significance.

Discovering your Life's Vision and Personal Constitution

Conscious Incompetence
We have become aware of the importance of our Life's Vision. We are not yet sure about how to discover and go about planning towards the fulfilment of our Life's Vision.
Conscious Competence
We have learned how to discover our Life's Vision. We have also learned and become competent in setting congruent goals, how to create vision board, how to visionally plan, and how to get on the vision driven path to fulfilment.
Unconscious Competence
We have developed the knowledge and skills related to our Life's Vision, and we are able to unconsciously follow through and succeed, we have become the master of our own destiny.

Table 6.5 – Four Levels of Vision Competence

Chapter 7
Four stories on Life's Vision

Four days passed and I was still writing more pages on the topic of Values and the relationship with our Life's vision. I had breakfast earlier that day and spent about two hours writing out all the notes from the discussion with Dr. Competence on values.

I heard the phone ringing. When I reached the phone, I could see Dr Competence's name on the screen. I thought, maybe he had some good news to share. I picked up the phone:

Homi: Hello, how are you?

Dr. Competence: Thanks, I am fine.

Homi: That is great.

He just continued his conversation:

Dr. Competence: This afternoon, I am going to a city about 150 Kilometres away.

Homi: Are you driving or going with a group of people on the University's shuttle?

Dr. Competence: I am driving, so I am asking you to come with me if you like.

Homi: Well, I have been writing, and I can leave the writing for tomorrow to continue. I mean I'd like to come.

Dr. Competence: I thought you might be interested in learning about the rest of my life story while we are on the short journey.

Homi: What about discussing chapter 7?

Dr. Competence: We will get to that, too, if there is time. In fact, we have a two-way trip, and each leg of this trip takes about a bit more than 2 hours.

Homi: Great, I am interested in hearing the rest of your story. It was some time ago when we were last discussing it.

Dr. Competence: Good, then get everything you need in a backpack and be ready in front of your house in approximately a couple of hours. I will send you a message when I leave. Bring your laptop if you want to continue writing while I am not with you.

Homi: How come?

Dr. Competence: Because there is a gathering that I have to chair for two days, tonight it is about a couple of hours, but tomorrow is all morning. We will be back tomorrow after lunch.

Homi: In that case, I will bring my laptop. Where will we stay overnight?

Dr. Competence: The university has already booked an executive suite for tonight; it has two rooms, and you are staying there with me.

The Directional Vision Board and its significance

Homi: That is fine, I did not expect that, but I am still interested in coming along.

Dr. Competence: Okay then, see you in a couple of hours

Homi: Okay, I better pack and get ready, see you.

I was packing for this unexpected trip. However, I was so excited because I would be with Dr. Competence for almost two days, and I thought this was great. I was almost ready when I heard the sound of a car approaching, and I guessed it was Dr. Competence. Shortly afterwards, I heard a car horn, and I knew it was him, so I grabbed my laptop and backpack and dashed out of my house. I locked the door and found Dr. Competence talking on his phone. As I was approaching his car, he stopped talking on his phone and told me to put everything in the trunk, which I did, and then I opened the front door and sat next to him. I waited for about one minute in silence while he was laughing and conversing with the guy on the other side. Shortly his conversation ended.

Dr. Competence: Hi, thanks for coming on this trip on such short notice. Are you ready? Can we go now?

Homi: Yes, we can.

Dr. Competence: Great.

He started the car, and we were on this unexpected journey.

Soon, we passed all the city streets, and we were on the road to our destination when Dr. Competence started to share his life story, which he had not finished last time with me.

Dr. Competence: The city we are going to is high in the mountains with lots of great views. As you know, I love nature, when the university asked me whether I would like to go on this trip I agreed, because these mountains are famous for their rainforest status, beautiful, lush green vegetation, and peaceful surroundings.

Homi: What is the event about?

Dr. Competence: It is about how we can be competent in life, work, and business.

Homi: Anything about Life's Vision?

Dr. Competence: It will reference Life's Vision

Homi: What will the participants do?

Dr. Competence: Participants come up with their projects that they want to be competent in implementing and learn how this is possible.

Homi: How?

Dr. Competence: It takes two days to become competent in what they are planning to do or want to achieve. Briefly, we go through some activities to understand the components of knowledge, skills, action, focus and strategies for every goal we set and how to work precisely to fine-tune the efforts to produce the best results.

Homi: That is very interesting. Is this for everything we do that we like to get our best results in?

Dr. Competence: Yes, in everything we do. For example, let's say we are working on the maintenance and preservation of the Rain Forest. In this case we need to have knowledge of the area, the natural elements, from the soil, water resources, rain, climate, trees, vegetation and animal habitats, weather, and the local people. Then we need to look at what skills, values, strategies and focus we need to use in an integrated manner, as well as what actions we need to maintain on a continuous basis, factoring the changes in the climate over the period we are planning for.

I was enjoying the scenery as Dr. Competence was driving. On my right I could see the valleys, green and vast, with patches of trees here and there. On the left was a mountain full of green bushes up to the top, and big rocks peeping through some trees. While we were driving through the spiral road, I saw some breathtaking scenery and landscape.

Homi: Well, that is very interesting. I hope you can share some of your experiences from this seminar with me on the way back.

Dr. Competence: Sure

Homi: What about your story? You left it unfinished.

Dr. Competence: I have four stories to tell you:

The first story is about what happened in the writers' meeting
The second story is how I wrote the paper on Competency Theory and DHM
The third story is about being kicked out of the university.
The fourth story is about taking the paper further to PhD level

Homi: These stories sound fascinating. Tell me about them.

Dr. Competence: Each of these stories contains a point to learn from about our vision

Homi: You already shared some portions of the first story, so what was the lesson from the first story?

Dr. Competence: The first story was what happened in the writers meeting. It is about finding your mission in life; where did I stop last time?

Homi: After encouragement from your colleagues, you applied to undertake your studies in the field of competence.

Dr. Competence: Yes, I did. You have already heard part of the first story and this is the rest. By the end of the first story, I applied, received confirmation of my enrolment and I officially became a university student.

Homi: So, what was the point of the First Story?

Dr. Competence: The Point was – When the opportunity comes, act because opportunities are the signposts to your Life's Vision.

Homi: Okay, tell me the Second Story

Dr. Competence: The second story was about how I wrote the paper on Competency Theory and the DHM

Homi: How?

Dr. Competence: I had two options to do my PhD. One was based on a simulation and the other was on cracking the competence code and figuring out how to train people to become competent and achieve competence. In the beginning I started on the first one as my supervisor had encouraged me to continue on this path which was easier for him. My Life's Vision was to become Dr. Competence by creating a method to teach competence.

Homi: Why creating a method?

Dr. Competence: Because there was no method, and if my vision was to become Dr. Competence, then it must be me who cracks the competence code and creates the approach to teaching competence in a new way, together with solving how to develop competence in anything you desire to learn in life.

Homi: So, you were being pushed by the University?

Dr. Competence: Yes, and it was hurting me; it became painful to take it when I realised that they were pushing me in a direction that was not my Life's Vision. Because in reality, my Life's Vision was to create a method to enable individuals to develop competence in any topic, concept, job or business. I believed that this is why later I discovered I was capable of supervising what I was doing.

Homi: Great, fantastic story. What happened next?

Dr. Competence: I spent many late nights developing such a method for the first time. I created a new approach that became known as the Double Heuristic Method, the DHM.

Homi: Were you tired?

Dr. Competence: No, I did not feel tired, because I found my Life's Vision, I had a strong feeling about it, creating a theory of competence that did not exist was my passion. I discovered my Life's Vision which I had been looking for since childhood when I was in grade nine. I was feeling great. This was the second story.

What was the point of the story?

Dr. Competence: The point - Follow your Life's Vision, and be brave.

Homi: Okay, what was the third story?

Dr. Competence: The third Story was about how I was thrown out of the university.

Homi: Did they endorse what you did?

Dr. Competence: No, unfortunately not. The university criticised me because I stopped working on the application for simulation as a PhD topic and chose to work on a Theory of Competence instead

Homi: What about your second supervisor?

Dr. Competence: My second supervisor was supportive. He was from another university, and he could see the reality that the world needs these findings.

Homi: What happened then? Did they give you a second chance to discuss the issue?

Dr. Competence: Not at all; the university dismissed, and banned me, saying that the change was unacceptable, and they would not have the personnel to support my studies.

Homi: Did you accept their argument?

Dr. Competence: No, during this time, I continued to work with my second supervisor on this theory paper published that year. I presented at a big conference on Education.

Homi: Did it end there?

Dr. Competence: This argument dragged on. I called on a close friend, and we composed a compelling letter to the university's Vice-Chancellor to take me on.

Homi: What was their response?

Dr. Competence: I received a letter from the Vice-Chancellor saying they could not support my thesis and that I was out.

The Directional Vision Board and its significance

Homi: You must have felt terrible.

Dr. Competence: Yes, I did. My world turned upside down, but I had made my decision, I am not giving up on the theory of Competence, the Double Heuristic Method (DHM).

Homi: What was the point of the third story?

Dr. Competence: The Point was: Never give up and stick to your Life's Vision.

Homi: So, what did you do when your world had turned upside down?

Dr. Competence: This is the subject of the fourth Story.

Homi: Tell me about it.

Dr. Competence: The fourth story is about how I took that paper further to PhD level; the point was – I was determined to keep at it until I succeeded.

Homi: Your paper was already published, but you were out of university?

Dr. Competence: I had the paper in my hand and the book that published it. After so many months of late-night work, coming up with a breakthrough felt great. I had this paper and a bag full of articles and documents showing how much research I had done.

Homi: So, you had a breakthrough in the teaching and application of competence?

Dr. Competence: Yes, I had explored and researched, finding a solution to the problem of competence and how individuals can achieve competence, to become competent. I had a breakthrough in my hand, yet I was out.

THE RISE OF THE HUMANS

Homi: And you did not give up?

Dr. Competence: No, I did not give up. I started to search for other universities to which I could apply, to continue working to fulfil my Vision.

Homi: Did you get any response?

Dr. Competence: After applying to many universities, my endeavours finally worked out because one university asked me to see my work. I was very excited.

Homi: Did you go to see them?

Dr. Competence: On that day, I took my research paper, together with the book that was published my article, to see a professor at that university, I remember it was a Monday at 2 PM.

Homi: Did you arrive on time?

Dr. Competence: Yes, when I arrived, she saw I had a big briefcase, full of research papers. I was trying to open the case to show her some of my work when suddenly my briefcase flung open, and to my surprise hundreds of my research papers spilled out and slid all over the floor.

The professor asked, are these your works?
I said yes.

Professor: Show me the paper you have published.

I showed her the paper that was endorsed by the research professors and published.

Professor: Where is the book that you have published it

I presented the book to her, and she saw the published Article in the book

The Directional Vision Board and its significance

She showed interest in my work and asked for an electronic soft copy.

She showed interest in the Diagram illustrating the theory of DHM.

She asked, are these the components of competence?

Then, she asked me to give her a copy, and she printed it.

She went out to the printer to fetch the printout. I saw she was conversing with a gentleman.

I went out to greet this person.

She introduced the Dean of faculty to me. When we came back to her office, she said, "congratulations".

I was wondering what she meant.

She turned to me and said, "You already have done a PhD."

She said, "We can admit you, but because you have already done the PhD, you can enrol in a second PhD and apply the theory of Competence, the DHM that you have already done". In other words, as the method is already developed and documented, she suggested that I can now apply it practically in the new PhD study.

Homi: Thanks for sharing, but what was the point of the fourth story?

Dr. Competence: The point was –Never Give up on your Life's Vision

THE RISE OF THE HUMANS

Chapter 8
The Directional Vision Board and its significance

"If you are working on something that you really care about, you don't have to be pushed. The vision pulls you." – Steve Jobs

"Every time we set a goal that is aligned with our values, we have the highest probability of achievement" - Dr. John Demartini

It was a Thursday and Dr. Competence and I decided to have coffee at a shopping center close to my place. We agreed to meet near the bookshop, and chose the shopping centre to look around the various shops while discussing vision boards. As usual, I accepted the idea of meeting the next day. We agreed to meet at 10:30 AM at the coffee shop we both knew.

The following day, I was at the Shopping Centre a bit earlier. He was also early.

Homi: Good Morning to you; it is a lovely day.

Dr. Competence: Yes, it is sunny again, a great day. As you said, today we will focus our discussion on Vision Boards.

Homi: Yes, and as a matter of fact, I like the topic of vision boards.

Dr. Competence: Well, yes, it sounds great.

While walking, we found ourselves in front of a Coffee Shop. The aroma dragged us in. We ordered our coffee and sat down. Shortly, our coffee was served, and we continued our conversation.

Homi: However, it is essential to know the significance of the Directional vision board before we start?

Dr. Competence: The significance of a Directional Vision Board (DVB) is that it is decorated with your Arrow of Vision. By placing the Arrow of Vision at the centre of your vision board you give it the direction it needs. This direction guarantees fulfilment, achievement and the realization of your Life's Vision. By doing this, sincerely, you become unstoppable.

Homi: Before we discuss this great topic and delve into how to build a Directional Vision Board, we need to know precisely why we call it a Directional Vision Board.

Dr. Competence: A Directional Vision Board is a collection of images, drawings, words, text, photographs, pictures, affirmations and even collected sounds representing our goals that are integrated on one board and arranged in an integrated manner to set the direction of fulfilling our Life's Vision.

Homi: Wow! That is fantastic.

Dr. Competence: Because it has to do with the Life's Vision you have in mind? It follows the discussion we had that your goals are not the Life's Vision and vice versa.

Homi: Does it mean that if we want to create a Directional Vision Board for Gandhi's vision, we can place images representing Gandhi's goals in an arrangement to how he fulfilled his Life's Vision.

The Directional Vision Board and its significance

Dr. Competence: Exactly

Homi: Or, if we want to provide an example, we can build a Directional Vision Board (DVB) for Lilly based on an interview with her that represents Lilly's goals along the direction of Lilly's Life' Vision.

Dr. Competence: Spot on.

Homi: Then what about people who just put together a vision board annually?

Dr. Competence: Some people create vision boards and they set goals that have nothing to do with their vision, so they do it anew every year.

Homi: Why are the majority of these goals not achieved?

Dr. Competence: Because these goals are not linked to their Life's Vision. Hence, they are not empowered by their vision to achieve these goals.

Homi: Okay, what happens when we have created our vision board, in this new way?

Dr. Competence: When you have created your vision board in this new way;

- You feel excited,
- You feel motivated,
- You think you are inspired, stimulated and it supports your vision.

The vision board that is created this new way:
- Becomes a piece of art,
- Becomes a creation,

- It shows the vision-driven path that you are going to take.
- It is not only a source of inspiration, but it also becomes the inspiration itself.
- Not only that you like it, but you also feel you love it.
- It will impress you and fire you up and, whoever comes in contact with it.

Homi: How does it affect us?

Dr. Competence: It has a subliminal effect, and as you see it every day, you gradually are influenced into actions towards fulfilling your Life's Vision.

Homi: Do all the goals on DVB motivate us to move?

Dr. Competence: The goals not contributing to our vision, and not underpinned by our values, are not powerfully motivating you. Even if you achieve these goals, the excitement fades away and after a few days, or weeks; they lose their motivating grip/power and are gradually pushed aside.

Homi: What happens if we identify those goals and remove or replace them with some empowering and relevant goals underpinned by our values that are vision-driven?

Dr. Competence: Then, our Vision Board becomes the motivating powerhouse that moves us. Because our vision board now consists of those goals that are contributing to our vision, every goal becomes a stepping-stone driving us towards our fulfilment, the fulfilment of our Life's Vision, the reason we are here in this life. This is how powerful it becomes.

The Directional Vision Board and its significance

Homi: Wow! This is amazing.

Dr. Competence: Indeed, and amazingly, the goals that are contributing to our Life's Vision stay alive, motivating us, and inspiring us to move along the vision-driven path. More of this will be clear to us after we pay attention to the real stories and examples in your life, the people around us, and the lives of others who have followed their Life's Visions.

While I was enjoying both the coffee and the discussion, I asked:

Homi: Everybody has some kind of vision, or a Life Vision. Some may know it, and those who know it may not articulate it or create vision boards, but some do. What are your thoughts on this situation?

Dr. Competence: Because this world operates within a hierarchy of vision, our progress in this life depends on our Life's Vision, that is why we need to discover it, articulate it, create a vision board for it, go for it, and fulfil it. As we engage in these activities in our life, which are in congruence with our Life's Vision, we start to be lifted up, and feel we are rising as human beings, especially when we are applying the Rise of The Humans Framework (ROTH).

Homi: Can we also follow our vision when we work for our business or while we have a job and work for someone else?

Dr. Competence: Well, let me clarify. You either must have a Life's Vision which is starting something new, or improving on something that is already ongoing, or a completely new original vision. Alternatively, you may find your vision within a bigger vision of someone else's, a leading vision. In other words, you may be pursuing a smaller vision within that bigger vision, in that way, you may realise the fulfilment of your own vision. Because when you found your vision, you also found that your Life's Vision is similar to someone else's vision that is ongoing.

Homi: Does this hierarchy of vision serve humanity?

Dr. Competence: Yes, it does, in many ways and via many means. Plus, it is within this hierarchy of visions that we make a living.

Homi: What happens if we are not in this hierarchy of vision?

Dr. Competence: Whilst without a vision, you can't function in this world and in this life.

Homi: What do you mean?

Dr. Competence: Well, without finding our Life's Vision, we are either lost, or feel dismayed in some ways, in our lives. We thirst for fulfilment, but the achievement of this fulfilment becomes a mirage.

Homi: Why is this the case?

Dr. Competence: It is because our progress in this life is based on our Life's Vision. Our Life's Vision tells us where we are going, what we are doing, and what we can expect, which is comprised of several goals that are represented by an image, or multi layered goals on our vision-board that serve our vision, taking us towards its fulfilment.

Homi: What does that mean, multi-layered?

Dr. Competence: It means that our vision board may have a number of goals and that achieving one goal facilitates the achievement of all these goals to take us on a journey which

The Directional Vision Board and its significance

leads to the fulfilment of our Life's Vision. So, our vision is fulfilled by achieving the goals that our Vision-Board represents.

Homi: Do you mean even if we work, we need to have a Vision-Board?

Dr. Competence: Yes, as I mentioned before, whether we have a job or work for ourselves, we need to have a vision-board. Whether we are serving the bigger vision of someone else and at the same time serving our own Life's Vision, within that larger vision, or we have a totally independent Life's Vision of where we are heading in life, we have several goals that serve and fulfil that vision.

Homi: So, do you mean whether we are working for ourselves or someone else, we need to have a vision-board?

Dr. Competence: Yes, either way you have several images that represent those goals, and those goals collectively serve the Life's Vision that you cherish, and you are moving towards.

Homi: How should our vision-board look?

Dr. Competence: Our vision-board should look like an aerial view of our vision driven path. In other words, it has a direction. It is like a vision driven path that we are going to be on, in order to fulfil our vision. It is the ultimate inspiring vision that we have for this life of ours.

Homi: How do we find meaning if we just have a job?

Dr. Competence: We are vision oriented, and vision driven. Our vision is consists of a number of goals that are underpinned by our values. Our life is meaningful when we are living in congruence with our Life's Vision underpinned by our primary values. We either find meaning in pursuing our own Life's Vision, or we may find meaning in serving some bigger vision that somebody started, provided it closely matches our own Life's Vision and our set of primary values.

Homi: Is this what happens when a number of people find commonality or similarity between their Life's Vision and a company already progressing with an ongoing vision?

Dr. Competence: Exactly! This can happen. If we are the company and could bring those people with the right vision that helps our advancement, we have taken a step up on the vision driven path with a huge advancement. The bigger and more exciting and inspiring a vision is, the more it attracts other people to join in and become a swarm of people who are moving towards a bigger more prosperous vision that brings prosperity to the whole swarm.

Homi: Can you make it clear with an example?

Dr. Competence: For example, while Steve Jobs was serving his vision or creating a new brand of Apple computers, smart phones, or iPods, those who were working for Apple were serving his vision at the same time, if their own Life's Visions were close to Apple's vision.

Homi: And if not?

Dr. Competence: However, if their visions were not in line with Apple's vision and they had their own Life's Vision, while assisting the Apple vision, they would be incongruent.

Homi: But we also want to find contentment, so what happens if we feel meaningful but not content?

The Directional Vision Board and its significance

Dr. Competence: It is impossible, we feel happy and content when we find meaning, either within that larger vision of someone else or within our own vision. If we do not feel that, it does not make sense and we do not have this feeling of meaningfulness, we do not feel happy and we do not feel the sense of fulfilment.

Homi: Is the feeling of fulfilment an instant feeling that can come and go?

Dr. Competence: Fulfilment is not something that just happens sometime in the future instantly. It is a continuous feeling as we go about achieving the goals along the fulfilment of our vision.

Homi: How do we know we are feeling the fulfilment you are talking about?

Dr. Competence: When we feel fullfiled, we are feel that we are rising as a human, we feel we are rising high, we feel great, we feel excited about our direction because all these give us direction. So, when we feel we are rising higher, we know it is a sign of fulfilment, as we feel we are rising, we develop a sense that we can fly with the virtual wings we have created.

Homi: What can the feeling of fulfilment give us?

Dr. Competence: The sense of fulfilment gives us happiness and a feeling of contentment as this feeling continues all through the vision driven path that we are on for our journey of fulfilling our Life's Vision.

Homi: Does this feeling of fulfilment change?

Dr. Competence: The sense and feeling of fulfilment will be a consistent feeling, and if at times we feel perplexed by it, we will bounce back. It is this feeling that produces joy and happiness, contentment and a sense of certainty and confidence that we are on the right track towards that fulfilment.

Homi: Do we get this feeling of joy, certainty, and confidence, when we look at our vision board?

Dr. Competence: Sure, our vision board inspires us, because it portrays our journey to fulfilment, as a picture or collection of pictures, etc. It is so inspiring that it moves everyone towards the fulfilment of their Life's Vision.

Homi: Where can we place our vision board to be more inspiring?

Dr. Competence: The most inspiring place for our vision board is in any room in which we can be inspired by it in the morning and evening.

Homi: What happens if we have already created our vision board?

Dr. Competence: If you already have a vision board, you need to sit down and rethink and reflect on the principles we discussed here and rearrange your vision board based on the principles we are still to cover in this chapter. I think we better focus on some questions and answers on how to construct the Vision Board.

Homi: What are your thoughts on whether or not we should ask for the opinions of others before we build our vision-board?

Dr. Competence: No, we do not need to talk and ask for others' opinions, it is our Vision Board, not theirs. Do not let

The Directional Vision Board and its significance

anyone influence you about what you are going to set on your vision board.

Homi: Why should we avoid the influence of others?

Dr. Competence: Because, what needs to influence you in creating your vision board is you. It is your Life's Vision; no-one deeply knows your Life's Vision but you.

Homi: Why do we create our vision board mostly with images?

Dr. Competence: It must be visual, the images or text you put on the Vision Board must jump at you, must talk to you, must inspire you, must move you. Also, it must be visual, because it is about the goals and stages you are going through on the vision driven path to fulfil your life' vision.

Homi: It is said that a picture conveys a thousand words. Does this have something to do with our vision board?

Dr. Competence: Exactly, the images you choose must be pictures that convey a thousand words to you, so carefully choose your vision board pictures. It is about your dreams, your Life's Vision, so make sure each image you put on the vision board echoes a thousand words about you and your vision and no one else. Pictures that are worth a thousand words for you must be on your board.

Homi: How do we start to create the Vision Board?

Dr. Competence: The first thing we need is a large paper, may be an A3 size paper, that will do. Or if we like, we can set up an actual board on the wall, somewhere that is visible to us day and night.

Homi: Then what?

Dr. Competence: Then we need our vision board to allow us to visualize our ideal goals. It is better to use photos of goals that are important to us on our vision board, to help us achieve our goals on a daily and regular basis.

Homi: Where can we find these images?

Dr. Competence: We can go through some magazines to find images. We can take some photos with our camera/digital camera on our phone. When we find an image we like in a magazine, we can take a photo of it. If we see even some large text or words that make sense to us, or that jump out at us, we can just cut out those pictures and words that we like and use them on our Vision Board.

Homi: How important is our Vision board?

Dr. Competence: The significance of the Directional Vision Board, as referred to at the outset, is that it is decorated with our Arrow of Vision right at the Centre, while all our goals used as stepping-stones are arranged on both sides of our Arrow of Vision. Nothing is more powerful for manifesting our direction than this.

Homi: Do you mean that our vision board reflects our ideal goals and dreams

Dr. Competence: Yes, it does, and as it is in front of us in a visible inspiring spot, it constantly stimulates our brain reminding us of our future.

Homi: What happens if, for example, we could not find images that represent our goals or what we would like to place on our Vision Board?

The Directional Vision Board and its significance

Dr. Competence: You need to create images that are bold and strong. For example, if you like a type of car, go, drive it, take a photo while you are sitting behind the wheel, show the smile and confidence you would have if you already owned it and feel the emotion and the joy it gives you. In other words, the photo must show the feeling that it has already happened. So that the picture reflects how you feel when you achieve that goal, and every time you see it reminds you of the meaning of your smile in that photo.

Homi: Which goals do we have to focus on more?

Dr. Competence: We need to focus more on those goals that contribute to your Life's Vision. The goals that make us advance on the vision driven path and ultimately to our Life's Vision.

Homi: What should our Vision Board sketch look like?

Dr. Competence: The ideal design and best format for the creation of a Vision board is provided here for the first time, refer to Figure 8.1.

Homi: What do we call this approach, and why is this format the best format for the Vision-Board?

Dr. Competence: As this new approach introduces and gives the user direction, it is called "The Directional Vision Board" (DVB). The focus of the DVB is our life's direction, based on our Life's Vision. It is a Vision Board with the direction represented by a BIG ARROW.

Homi: What does the BIG ARROW represent?

Dr. Competence: The BIG ARROW represents our arrow of vision that we have covered in the previous chapter.

Homi: But the arrow of vision was about values. Wasn't it?

Dr. Competence: Yes, it was. Remember that values are the underlying force for our goals. Our goals are underpinned by our primary values.

Homi: What happens if others want to influence you to set a goal that they would like to see on your vision board which is not a goal that we would like to set on our vision board?

Dr. Competence: When we start to think about creating our Vision Board, we need to understand that our goals have underlying values for us, in this new way, we feel relieved of the pressure of the world around us that wants to influence us about which goals to set.

Homi: What about our Goals and their relationship with our Life's Vision?

Dr. Competence: Whilst we follow our Life's Vision as well our directional vision board, which has been created in this way, our goals become the stepping-stones leading us to the fulfilment of that vision. Our life starts to change, influenced by our Life's Vision.

Homi: How does this life change benefit and affect us?

Dr. Competence: As a result of these changes in our life, we will find that everything in our life is filled with joy and happiness, peace and harmony, success, and abundance. This change will influence other areas of our life in a positive and constructive way.

Homi: Can you provide some examples?

The Directional Vision Board and its significance

Dr. Competence: Sure, for example, we will find that our communication with others around us becomes enhanced and improved and becomes more exciting, and that in all other areas of our life we start to show progress, growth, prosperity and abundance. All of this happens because of our vision and the goals we pursue.

Homi: Is our Life's Vision the only reason we set goals?

Dr. Competence: Goals are also set because unconsciously, they fulfil certain core or primary values for us.

Homi: Which ones of our goals fulfil our values?

Dr. Competence: Goals such as possessions, positions, degrees, etc. These items have deeper value beyond their price tag. This value correlates to our core values which in most cases are unconsciously or subconsciously linked to the goals we set.

Homi: What about the goals we set up on our vision board?

Dr. Competence: In most cases, the images of the goals that we stick on our vision boards have subconscious value linked to the things we would like to possess, or which we plan to achieve.

Homi: So, why is it that some goals are not achieved even though they are set on the vision board?

Dr. Competence: Goals are not achieved because the hidden and subconscious core values attached are either not strong enough, absent, or have no underpinning value.

Homi: Could there be other reasons too?

Dr. Competence: Yes, it is possible that it was not a true core value, or that it was not congruent enough to achieve the goal.

Homi: When we do not achieve a goal, is it the goal or the values that are responsible?

Dr. Competence: I believe it is the values rather than the goals.

Homi: So, do you mean the achievement was not valued by us?

Dr. Competence: Well, the absence of congruence or a strong core value, does not spark the level of enthusiasm and dedication needed to achieve and realise that goal. Therefore, if the goals that we set on our vision board are linked to our true core values, they will be achieved.

Homi: What about the goals that we write to achieve?

Dr. Competence: Similarly, the goals that we write to achieve, must have an underpinning core value that empowers us to achieve them. However, we need to ensure that those core values are strong, true and congruent. The core values that we believe to be our true core values determine the way in which we set goals and achieve goals.

Homi: Why?

Dr. Competence: Because what we express as our core values may not be our true core values that we inherently believe to be our true core values.

Homi: Can you explain, how does this happen?

The Directional Vision Board and its significance

Dr. Competence: This disparity creates incongruence within us that could even cause some internal conflict. It is this aspect of goal setting that if not properly observed and done, leads to a weakening of the foundation of the goal and the grip on achieving that goal is weakened and ends in non-achievement.

Homi: Can you rephrase to make it clearer?

Dr. Competence: Sure, there are certain values that we truly believe in, which we operate from unconsciously. These are true core values which would be satisfied and fulfilled through the setting and achieving certain goals. Those goals, when realised, infuse in us a sense of fulfilment and satisfaction because they satisfy the true core values within us.

Homi: Why does this happen?

Dr. Competence: The reason is clear, while we are setting goals, we are guided by our unconscious mind to set goals that are supported by our true core values.

Homi: I see.

Dr. Competence: The reason goals are not achieved is because the hidden true core value underlying the goal was incongruent or was not strong enough to create the enthusiasm, dedication, and the drive to motivate us to achieve the goal.

Homi: What does the core or primary value do to the goal?

Dr. Competence: A strong and congruent core value that is underlying a goal, boosts commitment, dedication, and persistence for the goal to be achieved. This process gives us the enthusiasm and dedication which causes us to achieve that goal.

Homi: Do you mean it is the underlying cause of achievement?

Dr. Competence: True, the core values, we believe in, deep down within ourselves, determine the way in which we set goals and achieve goals. Core values are underlying causes through which we unconsciously desire to have certain possessions, positions, degrees and so forth. Our true core values are associated with our heart and emotions.

Homi: Can we think and find our values?

Dr. Competence: If we just think what our true core values are, we may be disappointed not to find them. There is no certainty that we will discover them that way. Rather, the way we feel about our true core values, leads us to discover them.

Homi: So, do you mean we feel the values, not think values?

Dr. Competence: Whenever we feel certain values to be our true core values, and we feel great, we are on the right track to find them. In this way, we naturally respond to our goals on our vision board by feeling the goals, loving the images, and get excited about them.

Homi: Do our values also have something to do with our calling?

Dr. Competence: Our core values unconsciously assist us, as through them we are attracted to our calling as well as to our goals. This is one of the ways we are attracted to our community and to the world around us.

The Directional Vision Board and its significance

Homi: If we just set goals because it is good to have goals, what happens?

Dr. Competence: If the goals are only set for the sake of just having goals, it becomes just a never ending and frustrating journey.

Homi: What is the relationship between our vision, our calling, and our values?

Dr. Competence: Vision is all about our calling, and who we are going to become, whilst our values are extremely relevant to our vision of becoming.

Homi: Does our set of values happen when we are in our teens or later?

Dr. Competence: We have adopted a set of values throughout our lives, which we have formed over the years. Our values, developed throughout our lives, guide us to make new decisions and set and achieve new goals. They are the underlying reasons why we choose to set and achieve specific goals.

Homi: What does achieving these goals do for us?

Dr. Competence: Achieving goals underpinned by our values brings us closer to who we want to become and helps us to move closer to fulfilling of our Life's Vision. Therefore, every goal that we have set and placed on our vision board has a fulfilling value underneath it, that holds it up and makes us achieve it, to consolidate the underlying value.

Homi: Do the goals and underlying values relate to some areas of our life?

Dr. Competence: There are specific values for all the areas of life that underpin the goals we choose to set in that area of life, such as personal growth, relationships, family, career, business, and spirituality. Focusing on one vision and set many goals to achive and fulfil our vision is better.

Homi: What do you mean by one vision and many goals?

Dr. Competence: This approach of one vision and many goals will help us to grow and achieve the uncertainties discussed in the first chapter. In this way, we set goals in all areas of our life to serve our Life's Vision because this approach gives us the direction specified in our Directional Vision Board.

Homi: Does it mean that the goals have links to our vision and values?

Dr. Competence: As we mentioned before, the goals need to be linked to our Life's Vision, whilst paying attention to the underlying values that bind and consolidate it in our life is vital.

Homi: Why?

Dr. Competence: Because goals are transitory, they can be set and achieved in a particular time, so they are time-bound, whilst our values with underlying and perpetual perspectives are tied to giving meaning to our lives through the fulfilment of our it Life's Vision.

Homi: Are these the goals set on the Directional Vision Board (DVB)?

De Competence: Yes, these goals are important to us. We can set these goals in all areas of our lives and ensure that they are based on our core values comprised of a mix of Propelling,

The Directional Vision Board and its significance

Sustaining, Lifting and Protecting values. These are then set on our Directional Vision Board (DVB), and as such they are among the goals we will achieve. This is illustrated in Figure 8.1.

Homi: So far, Vision Boards, as is practised globally, have only been about having a visual understanding of our goals.

Dr. Competence: True, but it is time for a change. The existing vision board design has lost its vigour. The Directional Vision Board (DVB) has to replace existing Vision Boards with a new structure globally. DVB is a vision board with a new dimension. It has direction based on our Arrow of Vision. A Directional Vision Board is a vision board that becomes meaningful and a source of inspiration and empowerment.

Homi: What happens when we give our Vision Board this new dimension which becomes Directional Vision Board (DVB)?

Dr. Competence: What happens is this: your DVB becomes a reflection of the direction you are taking in your life, based on your Arrow of Vision, and your Life's Vision. The BIG ARROW on the DVB represents the direction your Life's Vision is taking you and moving you along the Vision Driven Path.

Homi: Then what happens to our goals?

Dr. Competence: Our goals become congruent with our vision in this new way. On this basis, you set all your goals along your Arrow of Vision, the BIG Arrow, which is in the same direction as your life will to unfold. In other words, all goals are arranged meaningfully towards fulfilling our Life's Vision.

Homi: This is interesting. It is a brand-new perspective on Vision Board thinking that makes sense, works amazingly well, and it is exciting. The Directional Vision Board (DVB) comes alive in this new format. It talks to you, moves you, has direction, is dynamic, and it is all about advancing us towards our Life's Vision.

Dr. Competence: At present, around the world, vision boards have no direction, they require lots and lots of improvements.

Homi: Can you explain?

Dr. Competence: They need to be reviewed in light of the principles and materials we have presented here and reconstructed in the context of the DVB doctrine to make sense. Vision boards could be more active and dynamic.

Homi: How can existing vision boards worldwide become more exciting and powerful in the context of the DVB doctrine?

Dr. Competence: A new era of understanding will emerge by applying this new approach to review and reconstruct the existing vision boards with a BIG Arrow. Because, Directional Vision Boards (DVB) have a direction similar to our life, the Directional Vision Boards (DVB) are all about movement, like what our life should be about. This new approach, i.e., DVB is dynamic and not a stagnant vision board as you can see all around. The DVB approach is dynamic vital, in motion and involves emotion through the underlying values, and uplifting us as human beings to the

The Directional Vision Board and its significance

heights of fulfilment. An example, of a Directional Vision Board is as follows:

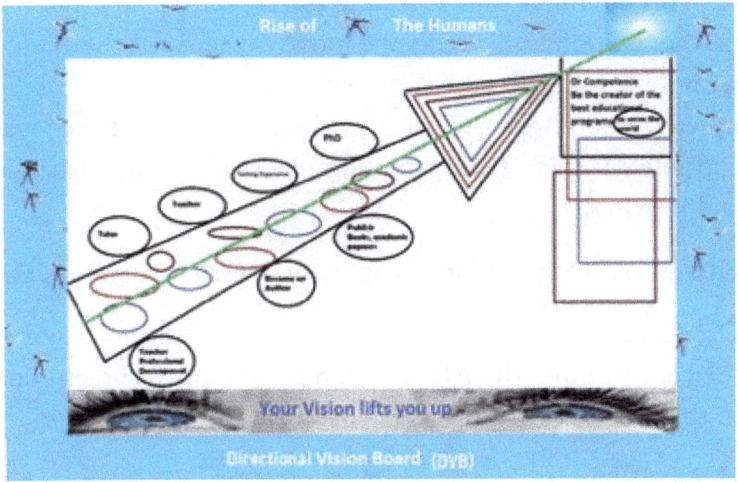

Figure 8.1 – The Directional Vision Board (DVB)

Homi: Why have you included eyes in the design of DVB (Directional Vision Board)?

Dr. Competence: It is true. The eyes revitalize and symbolize Helen Keller's famous quote and refer to people with eyes but no vision. Introducing eyes and vision into the design and presentation of the Directional Vision Board (DVB) emphasizes the point in Hellen Keller's quote. By including the eyes and direction in the DVB, this exceptional format, can transform the worst-case scenario that Helen Keller has portrayed into the best-case scenario, reminding us of what Helen Keller was trying to portray.

Homi: What is dynamic about the DVB (Directional Vision Board)?

Dr. Competence: The dynamic symbolism of the DVB is its BIG ARROW, which represents the Arrow of Vision, indicating the direction of our move into the future based on our Life's Vision. The goals are arranged in that direction, the frame is uplifting. It includes the rise of the humans; the sun on the top right symbolizes the move towards light and unity with our Life's Vision. The eyes at the bottom looking upward embody Helen Keller's reference on the topic of eyes and Life's Vision. This symbolism makes the model dynamic and moving.

Homi: What is the relationship between DVB and ROTH?

Dr. Competence: The Achievement Line is green drawn at the centre of the BIG ARROW, representing the green zone in the Rise of the Humans Framework.

Homi: Where are the goals arranged?

Dr. Competence: The goals are arranged on both sides of the achievement line. The Directional Vision Board (DVB) moves us and whoever comes in contact with it. The DVB uplifts us makes us rise, higher and higher, to the heights of fulfilment.

Homi: Does the achievement line on the Vision Board always need to be drawn at the Centre of the arrow?

Dr. Competence: Of course, it is right in the middle of the BIG ARROW, reaching the sun, the symbol of light. The DVB imagery could be so uplifting that the vision board becomes as robust as possible, to inspire and empower us with its subliminal effect.

Homi: Can you provide us with an example?

Dr. Competence: An example is provided in the following few pages.

The Directional Vision Board and its significance

Homi: If on the way to accomplishing our goals some unexpected incident happens, what do <u>we</u> do?

Dr. Competence: We need to be constantly flexible.

Homi: Why?

Dr. Competence: Because so many unforeseen circumstances could occur along the way. There may be something already in the making that we need to be aware of.

Homi: Okay, what do we need to do if such an unexpected incident happens?

Dr. Competence: As time passes, any of those unexpected events/things can suddenly pop up and occur to us. It may seem like an unforeseen pitfall or hinder our efforts, and we may need to adjust the route of our journey for a short while, and eventually get back to our vision-driven path again.

Homi: Is this why we need to be flexible?

Dr. Competence: Yes, that is why we need to be ready and flexible to deal with them as they arise, amend our DVB with the ultimate flexibility as soon as possible and be prepared for the next unexpected event.

Homi: Can we sum it up, please?

Dr. Competence: Why not. The conclusion is that the Directional Vision-board (DVB) is a mental picture of a condensed map, or our pathway of progress to our future success, where we fulfil our Life's Vision. It is a mental GPS map of our becoming, projected into our preferred futures. The DVB guides us to become whoever we are to become. DVB also represents our Arrow of Vision, which we studied in a previous chapter. The DVB is, in fact, the picture of our

Vision Driven Path. The DVB is the basis for visional planning, covered in the next chapter.

At the beginning of the book, we referred to Helen Keller. If you remember she mentioned that people who have eyes and no vision are worse than being blind. What she said inspired me to draw an approximate representation of her DVB based on her life. Her DVB is an excellent example to learn from.

Hence, we have gathered some data about her life in creating her Directional Vision Board (DVB):

In 1888, Keller started attending the Perkins Institute.

In 1894, she attended Wright-Humason School for the Deaf.
In 1896, she studies at Cambridge School for Young Ladies

In 1900 She enrolled at Harvard University.

In 1904, at 24, Keller graduated and received her Bachelor of Arts degree.

She was determined to communicate by lecturing.

In 1913 she published a series of essays on socialism.

By touching people's lips with her hand while they were speaking, she could understand what they were talking about.

She became proficient at using braille.
Keller visited 35 countries from 1946 to 1957.

The Directional Vision Board and its significance

In 1948 she went to New Zealand and visited deaf schools in Christchurch and Auckland.

The Directional Vision Board (DVB) for Hellen Keller was created as follows:

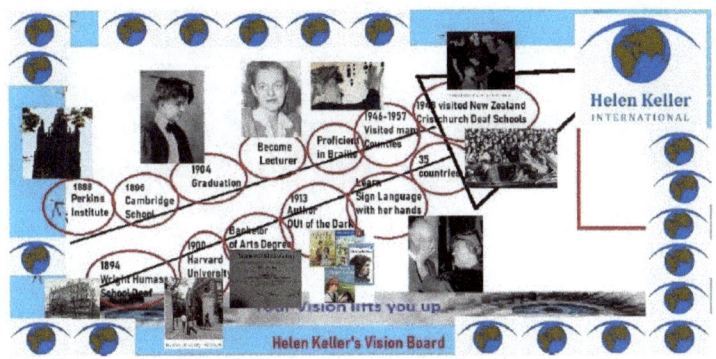

Figure 8.2 – Hellen Keller's DVB

Homi: This is so inspiring! As you mentioned, DVB is the basis for visional planning that is covered in the next chapter" so we may need to arrange a meeting in the next few days to discuss Visional Planning. Would you agree?

Dr. Competence: Sure, I suggest we meet at the bench in our favourite park.

Homi: I agree, we last visited the park some time ago; I like the idea.

Dr. Competence: That's okay with me. Shall we say Saturday at 10 AM?

Homi: That is fine with me. Okay then, see you on Saturday, and thanks.

Dr. Competence: See you.

THE RISE OF THE HUMANS

Chapter 9
Develop Mastery in Visional Planning

"A clear vision, backed by definite plans, gives you a tremendous feeling of confidence and personal power." — Brian Tracy, author, and motivational speaker

Saturday came, I got up early and sorted out the questions related to Directional Visional Planning (DVP). I knew that the Directional Vision Board is the basis of Directional Visional Planning, so I reflected on our discussion. I have already been writing about the DVB and almost completed the chapter but I knew I needed to edit my writing later. I was in my thoughts when I looked at the time and realised it was 9:30 AM. So, I got ready quickly, grabbed my keys, and drove to the park. I parked my car along the street and walked toward the bench that was on the other side of the pond in the Japanese garden park. This place was where I met Dr. Competence for the first time.

As I approached, I saw no one was sitting on the bench. I looked around and checked my watch, which was 9:55 AM. So, I went to the bench and sat there waiting for Dr. Competence. I knew he would be there on time. And I was right; he emerged from behind the trees wearing a blue shirt and a white pullover jacket. As usual, he had a relaxing friendly smile as he approached me.

Dr. Competence: Hi, there, how are you? You were earlier than me.

Homi: Yes, okay. I am early and enjoying the sun. How are you today?

Dr. Competence: I feel great; in fact, your book made me think a lot about planning today's topic.

Homi: Exactly right, it is about Directional Visional Planning

Dr. Competence: Yes, first of all, planning is the way to be prepared for what we want to implement and succeed in life. Being prepared ahead of time by planning has been a topic that many of the most successful people have emphasized. For example, Benjamin Franklin, *Founding Father of the United States,* stated that, "By failing to prepare, you are preparing to fail." — *Benjamin Franklin,*

Homi: In other words, we are preparing to succeed in fulfilling our Life's Vision through Visional Planning.

Dr. Competence: True. We will learn to become competent in Directional Visional Planning. In this chapter, we learn visional planning skills, how to integrate our visional skills with the knowledge of visional planning, and then take action to accomplish our Life's Vision on the vision-driven path. In other words, we will learn how to map out or plan out our vision and find the underpinning values, knowledge, and goals needed to be integrated into a plan whilst working with our Directional Vision Board (DVB). As Alan Lakein said, "Planning is bringing the future into the present so that you can do something about it now." — *Alan Lakein, author*

Homi: What are the Visional Planning components?

Develop Mastery in Visional Planning

Dr. Competence: Directional Visional Planning (DVP) is comprised of five major components:

- Knowledge that empowers us, and inspires us
- Values that propel, sustain, lift and protect us
- Goals that are vision-directed, and we have already set on our Directional Vision Board (DVB), to fulfil our vision by achieving them while we are on the vision-driven path.
- The Focus, that makes us Vision-Oriented, and self-directed to fulfil.
- The Strategies that cause us to become goal-directed

Homi: How can we illustrate these components and their relationships?

Dr. Competence: We use human face to show these components' relationships.

Homi: I wonder, why is a face used for visional planning?

Dr. Competence: There are a couple of good and wise perspectives herein using a face, to plan our Life's Vision.

Homi: Can you share these wise perspectives?

Dr. Competence: Sure, the first wise perspective, Ta Moko, is hundreds of years old.

Homi: What is Ta Moko?

Dr. Competence: Ta Moko is a face Tattoo worn on the faces of Maori men for hundreds of years as a reminder of their responsibility in life. Ta Moko on your face is a great honour. People who have Ta Moko are respected and it has always been a great honour. It is regarded as a treasure. It symbolises the responsibility of the person who have Ta Moko on their face.

Homi: So, Ta Moko is art too, is it?

Dr. Competence: Yes, Ta Moko is the art of tattooing the face. Why? The answer is that we need to face our life responsibilities. The wisdom of our Life's Vision is presented on our faces because it is our responsibility, and we need to face up to our life. Our commitment to our Directional Visional Plan (DVP) tattooed on our faces. Of course, in this exercise, we tattoo it on our photo, i.e., draw it only on our photo, with a memorable smile.

Homi: Which smile?

Dr. Competence: The unique smile showing how we would feel when our Directional Visional Plan (DVP) has been fulfilled.

Homi: So, what can we learn from this?

Dr. Competence: What we learn and the reason we do Planning on the face is that your Directional Visional Plan (DVP) is your responsibility, your visional plan is a treasure, your visional plan is respected, and it is an honour to have DVP and it is an honour to fulfil it.

Homi: Amazing, it touched my heart because it is as important as it is. So, we need to treasure it, and respect it, it is our responsibility, and we are honoured to have a Directional Visional Plan (DVP).

Dr. Competence: Exactly.

Homi: Okay, what other 'wise perspective' should we know?

Dr. Competence: Another 'wise perspective' is that those who go through the Directional visional planning (DVP), must remember to associate their five senses, as the planning unfolds. We need to put all our five senses on alert.

Homi: Can you expand and clarify?

Dr. Competence: Of course. We must understand that every one of our senses is associated with at least one component in Visional Planning. For example, the eyes are visual and thus are associated with our focus and values. The nose is olfactory and is related to our goals, where we can smell the pursuit of our goals and trace it to achievement. Our ears are associated with our strategies and the knowledge we hear to strategise. We coordinate our knowledge and strategy to make it work. Our mouth is associated with tasting and testing. Like when you are cooking a food dish, you taste at times, to see whether you are on the right track, and are going as you should be. Then, you may do some adjustments, such as adding salt, or spice, water, whatever may be needed, when cooking. Hence, our face is the best place to start Visional Planning.

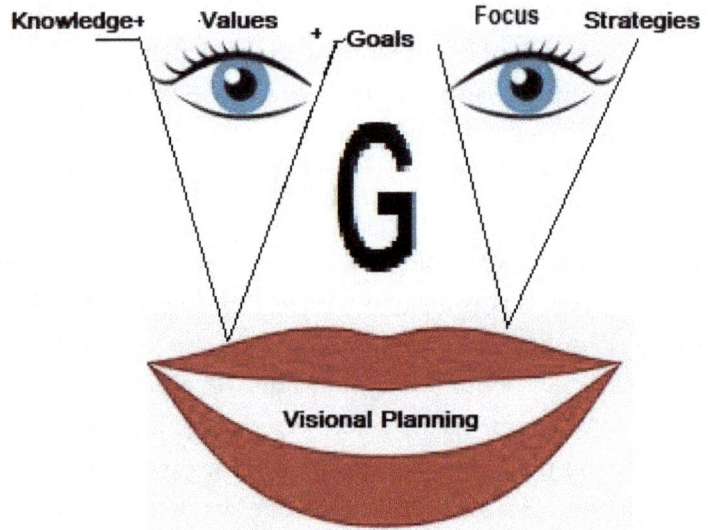

Figure 9.1 – The Relationship between knowledge, values, Goals, Focus and Strategies in Visional Planning

Homi: Are the goals the same goals that we have already planned on our DVB?

Dr. Competence: Yes, these are the goals that we have already planned for our Directional Vision Board (DVB).

Homi: What about knowledge?

Dr. Competence: We need to identify any knowledge, data or information that comes our way, to be filtered through our focus and processed wisely by us in our plan. We start with these five major components: Knowledge, Values, Goals, Strategies and Focus.

Homi: Is it true that one or more Values underpin our goals?

Dr. Competence: Exactly, each goal has underpinning values. In visional planning, there are two reasons why we set and achieve goals. The first reason is that it brings us closer to fulfilling of our Life's Vision. The second is that, at the same time, we are fulfilling our core values, comprised of primary and secondary values, which underpin that goal. Hence, in visional planning, we learn that the realisation of each goal has two underlying fulfilments. This is how powerful and vital this understanding is. Therefore, there is a crucial difference between this approach in goal setting and achievement and when individuals are setting goals just for the sake of setting goals, based on the argument that we should set goals because everyone else has. That is why many goals are not achieved by the goal setters. Those who do, unconsciously are fulfilling something much bigger than the goal, and in most cases, these are the underpinning values that are so fulfilling.

Homi: Why?

Dr. Competence: Because goals are material, the underpinning values are spiritual. It has to do with the meaning of the goal has for the individual that achieves it.

Homi: Is it about the meaning these goals have that drives people to achieve them?

Dr. Competence: Yes, definitely, according to Herbert Blumer, "Human beings act towards things on the basis of the meanings that the things have for them".

Homi: So, do we take action based on those meanings?

Dr. Competence: Correct, we can observe that we set and achieve goals based in of the meanings these goals have for us. And secondly, the meaning of goals in our life is based on how we associate our goals with our values.

Homi: Do you mean that this association inspires us to achieve our goals?

Dr. Competence: Definitely, and depending on how we see such associations between the goals and the underpinning values, results in those meanings.

Homi: What do we do when we want to decide on a goal? What happens?

Dr. Competence: What happens is this. We set goals based on our knowledge and the underlying values at the time. Our decision is guided by whether achieving our goals would benefit our progress on the vision-driven path.

Homi: Do you mean, when we realise that achieving a goal helps our vision, we can decide?

Dr. Competence: Yes, we can make a sound decision on the above basis. When we are confident that the underpinning values will be met by the goal we are setting we become sure that this goal is the right goal for our Life's Vision. Then when we place it on our Directional Vision Board (DVB).

Homi: Can you provide an example?

Dr. Competence: Okey, we can start with Gandhi's Tree of Vision to provide an example. To illustrate Gandhi's example, we first focus on Gandhi's case which we produced in a previous chapter, as follows:

Develop Mastery in Visional Planning

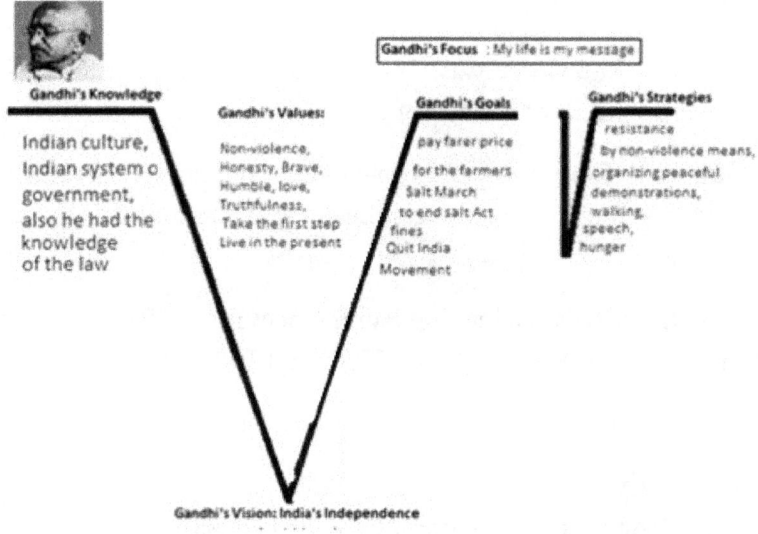

Figure 9.2 – Gandhi's Tree of Vision

Homi: Why Gandhi?

Dr. Competence: We chose Gandhi because he was an excellent example of an individual who fulfilled his vision of India's Independence. We do not exactly know about the details of his visional plan. However, only a few of his goals are listed in this illustration. This example is used for illustration purposes only regarding Life's Vision and its fulfilment.

Gandhi's goals: We used only a few for illustration purposes. He adopted specific core values that could have been the propelling values or Primary values for him: Non-violence, Honesty, Brave, Humble, Love, Trustfulness, Take the first Step, Live in the Present.

The items listed are:

Gandhi's knowledge was: Indian Culture, Indian System of Government, Knowledge of the law

Gandhi's Core values: Non-violence, Honesty, Bravery, Humility, Love, Trustfulness, Leading by Example, Take the First Step

Gandhi's Goals: Achieving Fairer Prices for the Farmers, Salt March to end Salt Act Fines, The Quit India Movement

Homi: What else do we need to complete Gandhi's Visional Planning?

Dr. Competence: To create the full version of Gandhi's visional planning for Gandhi we need his strategies and his focus:

Gandhi's Focus: My life is My message

Gandhi's strategies: Resistance by Non-violence Means, Peaceful Demonstration, walking, speech.

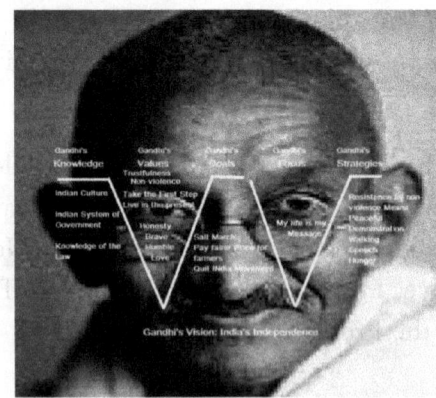

Figure 9.3 – First and Second Heuristics of Gandhi's Vision

Develop Mastery in Visional Planning

Homi: What can we learn from Gandhi's case and his Visional Plan:

Dr. Competence: We can learn from Gandhi's example that his Strategies to achieve his Goals worked well towards fulfilling his Life's Vision. Focus was to extend and convey his message, that "My life is my message" to Humanity. By connecting and linking his Strategies via his Focus, i.e., "My life is my message" he could then succeed in the achieving of his Goals. In other words, his Goals were supported by his Strategies, because of his Focus on leaving a legacy of being an example to the British, to Indians and to Humanity.

Homi: What about his Values?

Dr. Competence: Well, we can see how his Goals were supported and underpinned by his Values.

Homi: Is this what the visional planning is highlighting?

Dr. Competence: Precisely, Directional Visional Planning (DVP) emphasises that the Values connect what you know (Knowledge) to what you set to achieve (your Goals) which was the other aspect of Gandhi's Visional Plan. The Goals are assisted by the strategies we have formulated, and the underlying Values, which we have listed on our visional planning.

Homi: How does this apply to Gandhi's case?

Dr. Competence: In Gandhi's case, he acted on his Goals based on solid Values that propelled his Life's Vision and gave his vision the meaningfulness required to achieve it by all means. This meaningfulness is how those who never give up playing their role in the game of life to the complete fulfilment of their Life's Vision make victory and success a reality.

Homi: If you review Gandhi's Visional Planning, you will see the Goals are all listed at the centre in the visional planning, Why?

Dr. Competence: Because Goals are to be achieved as each Goal takes us one step closer to the fulfilment of our Life's Vision. They are stepping stones, to fulfilling our Life's Vision. So, these stepping stones are arranged right at the centre while connected to two sides, like the two sides of a coin.

Homi: What are these two sides of the DVP?

Dr. Competence: On one side, we need Strategies to follow and implement to realise the achievement of each Goal. In doing that, we also need a strong Focus that is meaningful to us, such as "My life is my Message" in Gandhi's case.

Homi: What about the other side of the DVP?

Dr. Competence: On the other side, we need to list the Values that give meaning to our Goals. Their achievement becomes the fulfilment of our Values, bringing us one step closer to our Life's Vision which is meaningful to us. Gandhi's values were: Non-violence, Honesty, Bravery, Humility, Love, Trustfulness, and Leading by example.

Homi: What about Helen Keller's Case?

Dr. Competence: Helen Keller was both blind and deaf. Her core values helped her to carry on despite the difficulties she faced her entire life. Helen Keller is example because she had no sight, but she had vision, a larger-than-life vision. She decided on her vision of helping and improving the cause of the blind and those with disabilities. Concerning vision and visional planning, she has a considerable number of thoughtful quotes. Among these quotations are the following she had on "Vision':

- The only thing worse than being blind is having **sight** but no **vision**.
- "Knowledge is love and light and vision."
- "Character cannot be developed in ease and quiet. Only through experience of trial and suffering can the soul be strengthened, vision cleared, ambition inspired, and success achieved."
- "The most pathetic person in the world is someone who has sight but no vision."
- "As selfishness and complaint pervert the mind, so love with its joy clears and sharpens the vision."
– Helen Keller

There are some of her quotes that do not directly but indirectly have to do with vision, with its multi-dimensional nature of vision

- "What I am looking for is not "out there," it is in me."
- "Believe when you are most unhappy that there is something for you to do in the world. So long as you can sweeten another's pain, life is not in vain."
- "No pessimist ever discovered the secret of the stars, or sailed to an uncharted land, or opened a new doorway for the human spirit."

- "<u>Death</u> is no more than passing from one room into another. But there's a difference for me, you know. Because in that other room I shall be able to see."
- "You don't love someone for their looks, or their clothes, or for their fancy car, but because they sing a song only you can hear."
- "Life is short and unpredictable. Eat the dessert first."
- "Happiness is the final and perfect fruit of obedience to the laws of life."
- "Walking with a friend in the dark is better than walking alone in the light." – **Helen Keller**
- "Life is a succession of lessons which must be lived to be understood." — **Helen Keller**

Homi: These quotes are so inspiring and uplifting. Was Helen's blindness an impediment to discovering her Life's Vision?

Dr. Competence: On the contrary, her blindness could not prevent her from discovering her Life's Vision and carrying it out to fulfilment. She overcame her difficulties and kept studying until she got her bachelor's degree, and then became a writer and speaker. Even though she could not hear or speak, she learned to produce sounds as close to her speech as possible to deliver outstanding speeches.

Homi: What was her intent in helping the cause of the blind?

Dr. Competence: Although she could not hear or see, she worked on her Life's Vision of helping the blind, she worked for the cause of disability globally, and she also worked for the cause of poor. She said that Humanity evolves by each one supporting and providing service to others, by loving and supporting one another.

Homi: How did she evolve as a member of the Humanity she was referring to?

Dr. Competence: Interesting question. Well, Helen Keller evolved from someone who truly knew hardship and adversity to one who successfully focused her time and energy on the worthy pursuits of growth, happiness, love, and compromise. She pushed her own (and society's) boundaries and became someone great.

Homi: What, in your view, can we learn from her, particularly from her Visional Planning?

Dr. Competence: What we can learn from Helen is immense because despite being deaf, blind, and having difficulty speaking, Helen Keller could to see and experience things in a way the rest of us can only dream. She could see the bigger picture. She may not have *sight*, but she had *vision*. She achieved more than most of us despite her difficulties and challenges.

Homi: What was Helen's ultimate message to us, to Humanity?

Dr. Competence: She said, that "Until the great mass of the people shall be filled with the sense of responsibility for each other's welfare, social justice can never be attained."

Homi: I knew how optimistic she was throughout her entire life. She also mentioned that we need to have optimism because "Optimism is the faith that leads to achievement; nothing can be done without hope or confidence."

Dr. Competence: Also, about difficulties in life, she mentioned that whenever we face difficulty in our life and find that the door is closed on our face, we should remember that "When one door of happiness closes, another opens; but often we look so long at the closed door that we do not see the one which has been opened for us."

Homi: What else can we learn from her example?

Dr. Competence: Helen has proved that we do not need to have eyes to see and be able to speak to discover and fulfil our Life's Vision. She is an inspiring individual and an excellent example for us who want to find and achieve our Life's Vision. As she said, "life is a succession of lessons, and the reason we are living this life, is to learn those lessons".

Helen Keller, living through the lessons of her life has proved that:

- We can stand up and speak even if we are disabled to utter a words
- We can discover our Life Vision even if we are unable to see
- We can fulfil our Life's Vision even if we are deaf

Despite her serious disabilities, she endeavoured and became well educated. She achieved certainty, success, open-mindedness, intelligence, understanding and she became helpful for the causes of the poor, disabled and blind. She realised many goals in her life, and here are just a few: attending the Perkins Institute, Cambridge School, Harvard University, earning her bachelor's degree, lecturing, publishing, mastering braille, traveling, and many, many more.

Develop Mastery in Visional Planning

Helen's Goals were: Wright-Humason School for the Deaf, Cambridge School for Young Ladies, Harvard University, bachelor of arts degree, lecturing, publishing books (12 books published), mastering braille, visiting countries around the world, and much more.

Helen's Knowledge: She said about knowledge: "Knowledge is love and light and vision.", Knowledge is happiness, Knowledge makes us learn true ends from false, To learn the cause of loftiness and abasement, To know the thoughts and deeds that make us feel great.

Some of Helen's Core Values: Relationships, Strength, Tolerance, Perseverance, Learning

Helen's First Heuristic of Visional Planning: Now if we integrate Helen's Goals with her underpinning values and knowledge, we can map Helen's first Heuristic of Visional Planning.

In the next stage of the Directional Visional plan, we need to find her strategies, and connect them to her goals, with the Focus she held in mind to achieve her goals.

THE RISE OF THE HUMANS

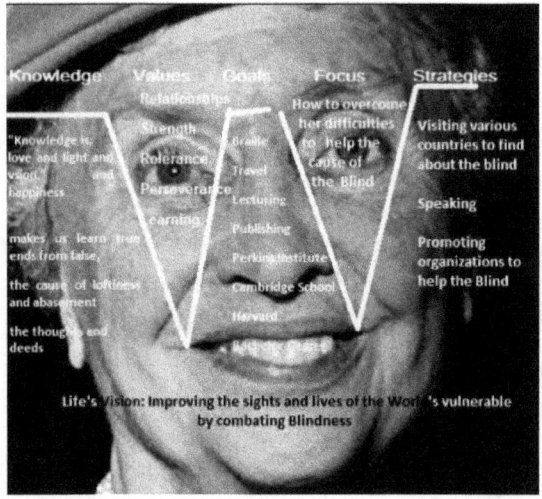

Figure 9.4 – First and Second Heuristics of Helen Keller's Vision

Homi: What can we learn from her smile?

Dr. Competence: One thing you will find is essential in DVP is the smile.

Homi: What do you mean by smile in this context of DVP?

Dr. Competence: Whoever completes the Visional Planning, first needs to take a photo with a Visional Smile.

Homi: What is Visional Smile?

Dr. Competence: A visional smile is a smile that you wear when you imagine, or visualize, that your vision has been fulfilled. It would be best to capture that smile with a camera, for the Directional Visional Planning (DVP). Like Helen Keller's smile, it is great for Visional Planning.

Homi: When did her vision come true?

Dr. Competence: Helen Keller vision became a reality, when in 1915, Helen Keller International was formed, a not-for-profit organization. She was appointed and accepted the role of Ambassador for the organization. Helen Keller International is dedicated to the cause of people who are suffering from blindness, poor health, and malnutrition.

Homi: As they say, what we do is written all over our faces, and is our responsibility. Ta Moko, a Maori tradition, also emphasizes this point.

Dr. Competence: Exactly, the face is the drawing place for Directional Visional Planning (DVP). In Helen's case, you can now see her vision on her face.

Homi: Yes, I can see, how beautifully it is written and what she achieved was more than impressive.

Homi: When we look at Helen Keller's Directional Vision Board (DVB), we see that she met several dignitaries to promote the cause of the blind and visited thirty-five countries.

Dr. Competence: Also, we can learn from Keller's example that the Strategies she used to achieve her goals, worked well towards fulfilling her Life's Vision. Her focus was to overcome her difficulties to improve the cause of blindness. By extending her message through visiting 35 countries, she connected to a global audience to promote her vision of improving the lives of the world's vulnerable and combating blindness. She was connecting her Strategies to her Goals, through her Focus: helping the cause of the blind. In this way, her Values were supported by her Strategies. On the other hand, her Values underpinned her Goals.

Homi: As we have learned from Gandhi's case, visional planning is about how our Values connect what we know (our Knowledge) to our Goals. Helen's Goals were assisted by her strategies but also by her underlying Values in her visional planning. Hence in her case, she acted on her goals, based on a set of solid Values that gave her vision a profound meaningfulness, which filled her life with joy. Her Values were necessary for the fulfilment of her Life's Vision.

Homi: What were the two sides of Helen Keller's Visional Planning Coin?

Doctor Competence: If you review Helen's Visional Planning, you will notice, once again, that her Goals are listed in the middle. There are two sides, one on either side of Goals. Our Strategies and Focus on one side and our values and Knowledge on the other side achieve each goal.

Both sides of the "coin" are significant to achieve the goal. Helen's Relationships, Strength, Tolerance, Perseverance and Learning Values were fulfilled, as she achieved consecutive goals to fulfil her Life's Vision advancing on her vision-driven path.

Homi: She was, and is, an excellent example for those on the journey of fulfilling their Life's Vision.

Dr. Competence: Okay, what about an example of a Visional Plan to clarify and make it easy to comprehend?

Homi: The best example is Lilly's case. She discovered her Life's Vision about three years ago. Every day passes she becomes more attuned to her Life's Vision. She has committed to fulfilling her Life's Vision.

Dr. Competence: That is great. Can you make a summary of her Life's Vision in few words?

Develop Mastery in Visional Planning

Homi: Yes, her Life's Vision is to become an international Tai Chi Messenger spreading the practice of Tai Chi around the world.

Dr. Competence: That is great, and you summarized it well. Okay, the next thing Lilly needs to do is to break it down into some stepping stones. What I mean her goals from three years ago through to some time into the future. Has she done that?

Homi: Of course. When I interviewed her, I asked all the necessary questions to discover her goals and more information that was necessary to know.

Dr. Competence: What are her goals?

Homi: Her goals are: Build the First Tai Chi Centre, improve her Tai Chi knowledge, develop her Tai Chi skills and practice, become a Tai Chi propagator and travel to 100 areas to promote the Taijiquan practice, and teach 1000 individuals.

Dr. Competence: Okay these goals are the stepping stones she will achieve on her vision-driven path to fulfil her Life's Vision. Each of the goals has a timeframe that needs to be realised. What strategies does she have in mind to guide her to achieve these goals? Has she thought about how to do it?

Homi: Of course. Her strategies are interesting. She mentioned that her first strategy is to be recognized as a Tai Chi teacher in China. She wants to do whatever is necessary to get this recognition in different cities, among many groups and several provinces. Then develop a new approach to teaching Tai Chi where she integrates Tai Chi philosophy, wisdom, and style in the practice of Tai Chi and uses it for her new venture. Her other strategies are interviews with masters, continuous training and learning from the masters. She has also arranged with her teacher, who already is running an international Tai Chi business, to consult with him before every move to fulfil her Life's Vision and to have him supervise her progress to the fulfilment stage. She also has a strategy to set up a new Tai Chi centre or studio per year.

Dr. Competence: What is her focus?

Homi: Her focus is: Tai Chi is My Direction to serve

Dr. Competence: What are Lilly's values?

Homi: Her Values are exciting they are: Vision, Good Health, Success, Achievement, Money, Internationalism, Courage, Love, Loving and Taking the last step, refer to Figure 9.5.

Dr. Competence: Fantastic! And what sort of knowledge does she think she might have?

Homi: Her knowledge, or shall I say the items of knowledge that she thinks are necessary for fulfilling her vision on the vision-driven path are: Tai Chi Philosophy, Long Term Planning, Yin and Yang Balancing, Tai Chi Movements, Chinese Provinces.

Dr. Competence: Okay fantastic. Can you see that you complete Lilly's visional planning by simply doing the two Heuristics?

Homi: Of course, here we are: The first Heuristic of Lilly's Visional Plan is as follows:

Develop Mastery in Visional Planning

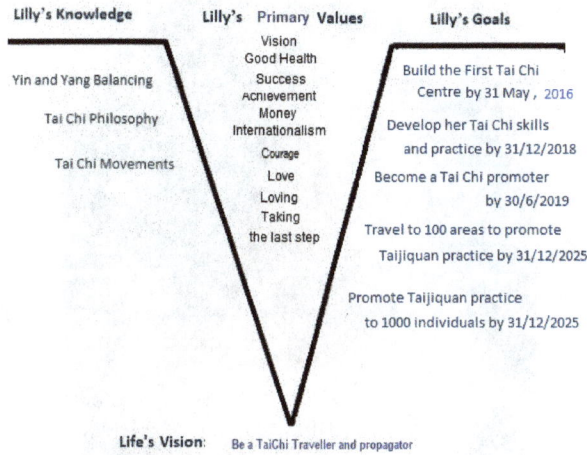

Figure 9.5 – First Heuristic of Lilly's Visional Plan

Dr. Competence: Here, you have used Lilly's Goals, together with her underpinning Values and Knowledge, correct?

Homi: Definitely. It is based on the data I got from Lilly in the interview. Although, only three items of knowledge are listed.

Dr. Competence: Okay. What about her Second Heuristic, when you expand the first one into the full spectrum of visional planning?

Homi: Well, as you know, we get a better understanding of the visional plan, when we look at the Second Heuristic.

Dr. Competence: Yes, I agree. So, can you provide us with a complete visional plan for Lilly's vision so we can discuss it and see its viability?

Homi: Of course, Lilly's second heuristic, including the strategies and focus, is as follows:

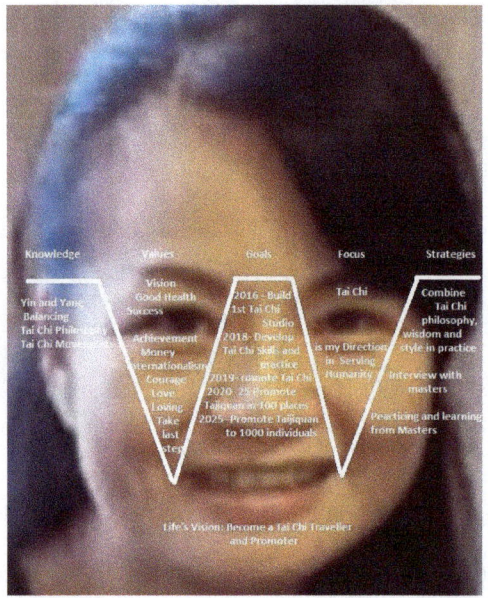

Figure 9.6 – First and Second Heuristic of Lilly's Visional Plan

She sees through the value of good health with one eye and serving Humanity through Tai Chi with her other eye to become a Tai Chi traveller and promoter, as her vision of becoming.

Dr Competence: It is essential to write a commitment statement and attest to it with our signature. This is necessary. **Homi:** Why?

Dr Competence: Because this is our Life's Vision and no one else will commit to it but us. It is our responsibility to fulfil our Life's Vision. Nothing is more critical than this commitment in our lives. Hence signing our name to our Life's Vision shows our commitment to fulfilling our own Life's Vision.

Develop Mastery in Visional Planning

Homi: Can you provide an example of Commitment Statement?

Dr Competence: Okay, something like the following:

I dedicate myself to my Life's Vision, enshrined in my Visional Plan. I truly commit to it and, at this moment, attest my commitment with my signature as a token of my foolproof pledge to never give up in implementing this Visional Plan to fulfil my Life's Vision successfully.

Homi: Where can we keep our Visional Plan?

Dr Competence: We must place a copy of our Visional Plan on the wall next to our Directional Vision Board.

Homi: Is this the last thing we must do in Visional Planning?

Dr Competence: The last thing we must do in visional planning is develop a plan of action for execution.

Homi: How?

Dr Competence: Each of our goals needs a plan of action. In the plan of action, we list the actions, which skills we need to use to take those actions, and concepts, topics, and knowledge concepts we will need to know about each action. In Lilly's example, she has to travel to 100 areas and propagate Tai Chi to 1000 individuals. The following Figure illustrates how her first goal was planned to 'Build or set up her Tai Chi Centre'.

THE RISE OF THE HUMANS

Figure 9.7 – Lilly's Action Plan for her goal – her Tai Chi Centre

On this basis, every goal has an achievement date, on the visional plan. In addition, it requires a dated action plan with a commitment day. Every action needs the date of implementation. It is essential to allocate a month for the achievement of a goal. If some goals need more or less time this needs to be specified. In the above example, Lilly planned her first goal to be carried out in May 2016.

Homi: Four more examples of Visional Plans are provided: Master Teacher, Liu Yong from China, Jack Ma, a Chinese Tycoon, Steve Jobs, Apple Founder and Mark Zuckerberg, Facebook and Meta Founder as follows:

Liu Yong

Knowledge: Opening our hearts to wisdom, Tai Chi Philosophy, Tai Chi Balance, Tai Chi Movements, Taijiquan

Develop Mastery in Visional Planning

Values: Vision, Health, Happiness, Equality, Joy, Harmony, Altruism

Life's Focus: Ascend unceasingly

Life's Strategies:

Use lots of personal effort,

Progress in process of learning,

Find more like-minded people,

Take advantage of right place principle,

Start from small goals to big goals

Goals:

2019: Set up a Tai Chi Health Centre in Guilin

2020: Online Launch of all Tai Chi Teaching Videos

2021: Publish 3 Books on Tai Chi teachings

2022: Accept Tai Chi Recruits (3rd Batch)

2024: Holding a Tai Chi Summit of 1000 to 2000 people

2025: Global Tai Chi Speech Tour

2026: Hold a Grand Tai Chi Exhibition and accept new Recruits (4th Batch)

2027-2028: Globalization of Tai Chi Culture

Vision: Global Master of Tai Chi – promoter of Peace, Health, Happiness, and Wisdom through Tai Chi

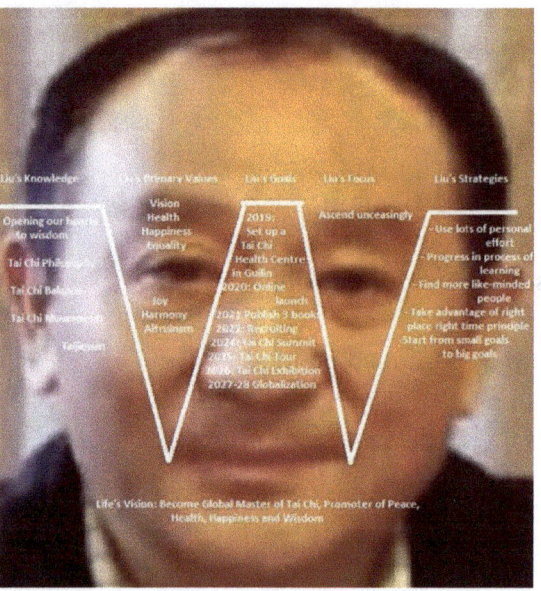

Figure 9.8 – First and Second Heuristic of Liu Yong Ten's Visional Plan

Jack Ma

Jack Ma was born on 10 September 1964. He is a Chinese business magnate, investor, politician and philanthropist. He was the co-founder and executive chair of Alibaba Group.

Ma has always been a strong proponent of an open market economy.

As a prominent business figure, Ma has always been seen as a global ambassador for Chinese business and is listed as one of the world's most influential people. He has been a role model for start-up businesses. He was ranked second in the annual World Greatest Leaders list by Fortune.

Develop Mastery in Visional Planning

On the 10th of September 2018, He announced that he will retire from Alibaba to pursue education. On 10th of September 2019, he stepped down from his role at Alibaba.

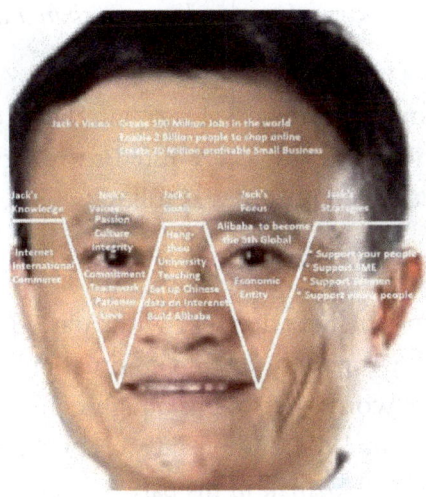

Figure 9.9 – First and Second Heuristic of Jack Ma's Visional Plan

Steve Jobs

Another great example is Steve Jobs Life's Vision, the co-founder of Apple Corporation.

Steve Jobs was intelligent but directionless, looking for his Life's Vision many years before he discovered it. Hence, is a perfect example for us to draw on based on his life experience. According to biography.com Steve Jobs was smart but directionless:

> "*Born in 1955 to two University of Wisconsin graduate students who gave him up for adoption, Jobs was smart but directionless, dropping out of college and experimenting with different pursuits before*

THE RISE OF THE HUMANS

> *co-founding Apple with Steve Wozniak in 1976. Jobs left the company in 1985, launching Pixar Animation Studios, then returned to Apple more than a decade later."*

For illustration purposes, a brief summary of his goals, aspirations, focus and values are listed to reflect his Visional planning for learning purposes as follows.

Steve Jobs' significant goals were: In 1974, Jobs took a position as a video game designer with Atari. Several months later he left the company to find spiritual enlightenment in India. In other words, he sought enlightenment by studying Zen Buddhism in 1974. When he was 21, he started Apple Computers with Wozniak in his parents' garage.

In 1980, his company, i.e. Apple Computers, with a market value of $1.2 Billion became a public company. In 1984, Apple Macintosh was a breakthrough and was released to the market. The following year, in 1985, because of some arguments between the board of directors, Steve Jobs left the company and started a new hardware and software company named Next Inc. In 1995, the Company, Pixar produced the film 'Toy Story', the first 3D computer-animated film. 2 years later in 1997 Steve Jobs returned to Apple Company and started his work as a CEO.

His Vision was to put a computer into the hands of everyday people. This vision was a shared vision with Wozniak.

Steve's focus on design is very interesting: Design is not just what it looks like and feels like, design is how it works. Steve

Develop Mastery in Visional Planning

Jobs' strategies and values are extracted from the internet, as an example to illustrate Visional Planning.

Steve Jobs Strategies were: He had extremely high expectations. He challenged himself -- and the people around him -- to work smarter, work longer, and work harder so he, and they, could accomplish everything they dreamed possible.

Values:

- Core value of Apple: People with **passion** can change the world for the better
- People who are crazy enough to change the world, are in fact the ones who do it.

Core values are what support the vision, shape the culture, and reflect what the company values. They are the essence of the company's identity the principles, beliefs, or philosophy of values.

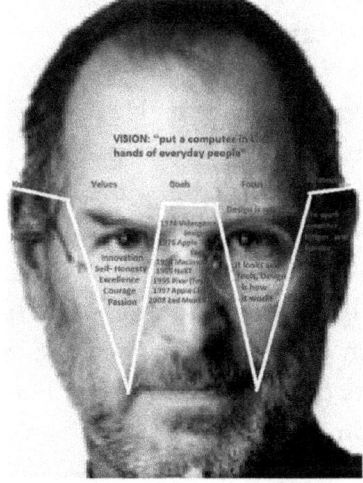

Figure 9.10 – First and Second Heuristic of Steve Jobs's Visional Plan

Mark Zuckerberg

Mark Zuckerberg, co-founder and CEO of Facebook, a social networking website, was born on May 14, 1984. He enrolled at Harvard University in 2002 after attending Phillips Exeter Academy. Then, Mark launched thefacebook.com on February 4, 2004. A year later, he renamed thefacebook.com to Facebook.com as an online directory. Facebook was connecting students via college social networks. Half of the student body signed up within two weeks. He made the site available to other campuses nationwide with the help of his classmates.

It emphasised networking, where users could create profiles, upload photos and other media, and keep in touch with friends, friends of friends—what he called the "social graph."

In the summer of 2004, he moved Facebook's headquarters to Palo Alto, California. The venture capitalist Peter Theil agreed to give them seed money. Facebook received its first seed money in May 2005.

Since 2006, everyone has been able to use Facebook. With the vision of focusing on long-term impact and his famous mantra, "Move fast and break things," Zuckerberg and his team have achieved one of the most remarkable growth stories in corporate history, with 2.9 billion users accessing Facebook monthly. More than half the world's online population uses Facebook each month. In October 2021, Facebook changed its name to Meta to embark on the metaverse. The Threads social network was launched in July 2023 as a text-based conversation app.

Develop Mastery in Visional Planning

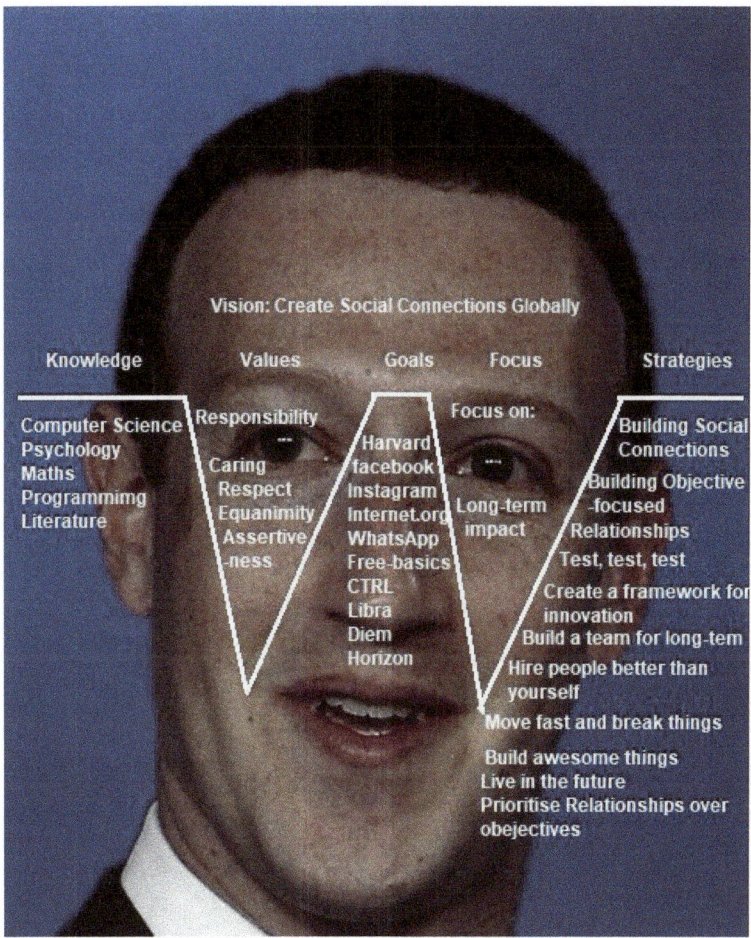

Figure 9.11 – First and Second Heuristic of Mark Zuckerberg's Visional Plan

THE RISE OF THE HUMANS

Chapter 10
Your Time Has Come

We must remind ourselves of the importance of the First Step without which nothing has ever been achieved. As Nelson Mandela stated:

"Action without vision is only passing time, vision without action is merely daydreaming, but vision with action can change the world." - Nelson Mandela

If we are to change the world, we must understand this last point that Nelson Mandela has emphasized, neither vision nor action in isolation can change the world. What can change the world is when Vision and Action come together. Yes, their combined forces inevitably can change the world.

"Vision is not enough. It must be combined with venture. It is not enough to stare up the steps, we must also step up the stairs." - Vaclav Havel

So, my dear friend, you have reached this page which means you have persevered to continue your journey on the vision-driven path to fulfilment. You deserve the medal of honour when you get to these heights. Now that you are here, you have one more thing to do. You need to take the First Step. As the First Step is taken, the second, third, and fourth steps will unfold in front of you, and in a glimpse, you will find yourself ahead in the journey towards fulfilling your Life's Vision.

So far, you have discovered your Life's Vision, completed your Visional Planning, planned your Goals and your Strategies on the Visional Plan, and you have planned several action steps for each goal. You might have heard the famous quote, "A Journey of one thousand miles starts with a single step". This quote proves how crucial the First Step is. Also, the following conversation indicates and further emphasizes the significance of this point:

Dr. Competence: If we do not find our Life's Vision and pursue something else instead, we will inevitably raise a conflict within ourselves throughout our life that leads to our regrets.

Homi: Can you explain how we can bypass regrets in our lives?

Dr. Competence: It is vital to find your vision and lay down the plan to fulfil it and take the first step towards its realization.

It means when you take the First Step, you do not fully foresee the second step, although you may have an idea as you planned. But as it unfolds, i.e., as it is happening, it brings several successes or some unforeseen and unexpected things you could not see when you started. As the steps develop, you will see what unfolding means. Sometimes you may not know what to do next, but you will see what to as it unfolds.

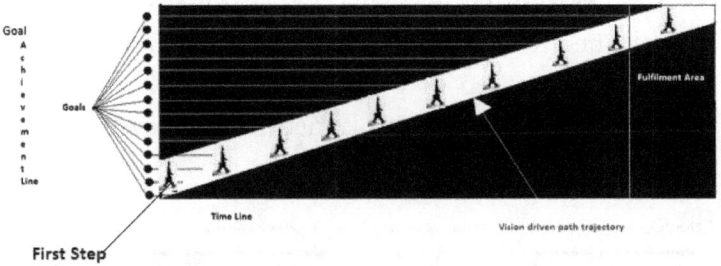

Figure 10.1 – Take the First Step

We learned that it is vital to take the First Step to realise our Life's Vision.

A conversation between Homi and Dr. Competence throws light on this topic.

Dr. Competence: Okay, so far, we have reached this stage which means that we have discovered our Life's Vision and planned it, and now we are at the stage where we need to take the First Step of our Visional Plan towards its fulfilment. Right?

Homi: Right, why are you emphasizing the First Step at this juncture?

Dr. Competence: Because vision without action is daydreaming. Taking action pivots around the significance of the "First Step".

Homi: Why is taking the First Step on the journey of fulfilling our Life's Vision so significant?

Dr. Competence: Because our Life's Vision comprises a number of goals, and each goal has a significant First Step.

Homi: Can you refer to an example to make it clear?

THE RISE OF THE HUMANS

Dr. Competence: For example, remember that the first goal Lilly planned to achieve was to set up a Tai Chi studio. The significant First Step of this Goal was, to "Make a list of specifications", which was planned and achieved by her as follows:

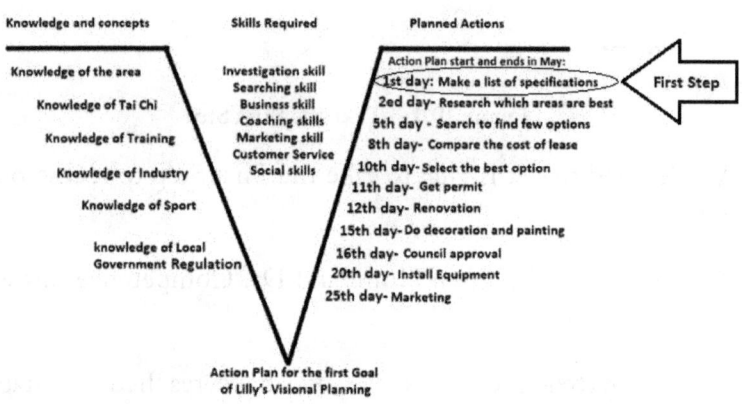

Figure 10.2 – Lilly's Plan of her first Goal indicating her First Step

It is magical as with your significant First Step you are about to trigger the unfolding of the remaining steps to the fulfilment of your Life's Vision, like a domino effect in which one leads to the next and so, and ultimately to fulfilment.

The time to take your significant first step is now. I am looking forward to seeing you at the top, and my best wishes and prayers are with you all along the way to the complete fulfilment of your Life's Vision. Bon Voyage.

Back to Questions of Certainty

So, my friend, you have come a long way in understanding the importance of your Life's Vision and its fulfilment. In

Your Time Has Come

Chapter 1, you assessed yourself with regards to how certain you were with a number of questions of Certainty. Now, the time has come to revisit Chapter 1 and assess your certainty once again, because you have improved a lot, much more than you could imagine.

Congratulations!

They say once the idea of an aeroplane was just an idea, now it is a reality. Once the internet was just an idea, and now is a reality. Most Life's Visions were just ideas and now they are realities. Core values like drive and passion, enthusiasm, perseverance, love, and talents of those engaged with these ideas brought their Life's Vision into existence. Your time has come. You have proved that you are one of them, and we are proud of you. And we are sure that you now have the knowledge and skills for turning your Life's Vision into reality in a way that will contribute to advancing your life, the people around you and the world. So, my friend, stay true to your Life's Vision even when the odds are stacked against you focus on the heights where you belong. We wish you the best of success on your journey to fulfilling your Life's Vision.

Yours truly, Dr. Competence and Homi.

THE RISE OF THE HUMANS

About the author

Dr Homi, known as Dr Competence, earned his master's degree in Management & Organizational Development from the United States International University (USIU), degree in Financial Management from the University of New England and degree in Education from the University of Southern Queensland. He acquired his PhD degree in Competency Based Training (CBT) from the University of Adelaide, SA, Australia. He is a Certified Trainer of Neuro Linguistic Programming (NLP) from Tad Games Co (USA). He is a Certified Practicing Accountant (CPA), (retired from practice).

Dr Homi is now the CEO of drcompetence.com and Doctor Competence and Associates Pty Ltd. He coaches individuals and business owners to prosper by discovering, funding, and fulfilling their life visions and making their impossible dreams a reality.

He has worked in the Private sector as a Chief Financial Officer (CFO), Auditor, Tax Accountant, and Management Accountant, as well as in the Public Sector, as a Leading Vocational Teacher (LVT). Dr Homi, taught for over twenty years, coaching Technical and Further Education (TAFE) students to achieve their goals and dreams. He is the father of Competencivism, Competency Intelligence, the Double Heuristic Method (DHM) and Competency Theory. Dr Homi has authored more than 20 publications and 17 conference papers on Competence, Competency Based Training (CBT), and Competency Intelligence.

His Book entitled, "Create Your Mental GPS", published in 2016, has already guided thousands of individuals to achieve their dreams. His message to individuals and business owners is: by applying elements of competence, as specified by the Double Heuristic Method (DHM), to what you do in your life or business, you will be able to succeed and produce real and satisfying results.

Dr Homi was inspired by the work of Gowin and Alvarez of the Stanford University in the United States on the 'V' Heuristic and created the DHM and applied it to competence and personal development. He was also inspired by the works of Bahaullah on the oneness of humanity, by Steve Jobs' approach to life, by Dr Bach's seven emotional categories and by Dr Jianping Zheng of China regarding the application of Bach flower essences.

www.ingramcontent.com/pod-product-compliance
Lightning Source LLC
Chambersburg PA
CBHW071332150426
43191CB00007B/707